Praise for *Discover Your EI*

CW01023414

'Emotional intelligence is the esse[n]...
business and for life. I worked witl...
brings the best of his teaching to this book. Part education, part
practical manual, but all delivered in Phil's trademark style –
accessible, funny and profound. Everyone who wants to do better at
their job – and better at their life too – should read this book.'

William Macpherson, Chair, Learning Curve Group

'Well, I did discover my EI and what a discovery. It was a revelation!
Meeting Philip Holder, back in 2007, was life-changing. Hiring
him as a coach for my MD at Adidas was the best thing I could have
done: the result was that we secured our bid as top-tier partnership
sponsor for the London 2012 Olympic Games!

Phil is a phenomenon! His book is like having a personal guru
in your pocket and reinforces everything I know about Phil – his
wisdom, his experience, his focus, his humility, his capacity for
joy, fun and laughter – these qualities ooze out of every page.
Easy to follow, practical applications to real-life situations and
"un-put-down-able", I enjoyed the learning all the way through.'

Yasmin Dewan, Inspirational Winners

'I met Phil 15 years ago and was struck by his ability to just "get" the
situation and what was needed. I have connected him to many in my
network, who describe him as the most intuitive person they know.
This book helps break down how he can achieve this. It holds lessons
and practical tips for us all to explore and enjoy what will ultimately
feed our growth.'

Tariq Ahmed, VP People, Achilles Therapeutics

'Insightful and inspirational, a collection of ideas and concepts that
provide a foundation and formulation with which to fathom and
navigate both our mental maps and the emotional blueprint of our
psyche.'

Catherine Robinson, Transformational Coaching

'Phil's book is like holding up a mirror to see the "inner you". I guarantee. You will discover a new understanding of yourself that will change you for the better. Enlightening, intriguing and a real page-turner.'

Roger Greenway, European Sales Director

'I have known Phil for many years as both a personal family friend and as someone whom I have called on many a time to coach me in my business challenges. Over the years, I have witnessed Phil's quest and passion for better understanding emotional intelligence (EI) and how he has gone on to use the "know-how" he has developed and matured, to help professionally, people in both business and those with other life challenges.

This book has been written with care and consideration as to how, by breaking EI down into meaningful parts, it can be better explained, improved and acted on to deliver more effective outcomes.

The inclusion of Phil's EI self-assessment tool provides a straightforward and thorough means to understand our own EI, identifying gaps which we can improve on through the activities Phil delivers in the book.

This isn't a book that you read and put away on the shelf to gather dust; it is a book to be kept on your desk and be referred to when you need to draw on your EI to improve performance, get better results and deliver a better you. A book that I strongly recommend.'

Vicki Shepherd, Head of Commercial – Central Government

Discover Your Emotional Intelligence

Pearson

At Pearson, we have a simple mission: to help people make more of their lives through learning.

We combine innovative learning technology with trusted content and educational expertise to provide engaging and effective learning experiences that serve people wherever and whenever they are learning.

From classroom to boardroom, our curriculum materials, digital learning tools and testing programmes help to educate millions of people worldwide – more than any other private enterprise.

Every day our work helps learning flourish, and wherever learning flourishes, so do people.

To learn more, please visit us at **www.pearson.com/uk**

Discover Your Emotional Intelligence

Improve your personal and professional impact

Philip Holder

Pearson

Harlow, England • London • New York • Boston • San Francisco • Toronto • Sydney
Dubai • Singapore • Hong Kong • Tokyo • Seoul • Taipei • New Delhi
Cape Town • São Paulo • Mexico City • Madrid • Amsterdam • Munich • Paris • Milan

PEARSON EDUCATION LIMITED
KAO Two
KAO Park
Harlow CM17 9NA
United Kingdom
Tel: +44 (0)1279 623623
Web: www.pearson.com/uk

First edition published 2021 (print and electronic)

ISBN: 978-1-292-37376-8 (print)
            978-1-292-37374-4 (PDF)
            978-1-292-37377-5 (ePub)

British Library Cataloguing-in-Publication Data
A catalogue record for the print edition is available from the British Library

Library of Congress Cataloging-in-Publication Data
Names: Holder, Philip, 1951- author.
Title: Discover your emotional intelligence : improve your personal and professional impact / Philip Holder.
Description: First edition. | Harlow, United Kingdom : Pearson Education Limited, 2021. | Includes bibliographical references and index.
Identifiers: LCCN 2021009971 (print) | LCCN 2021009972 (ebook) | ISBN 9781292373768 (paperback) | ISBN 9781292373744 (pdf) | ISBN 9781292373775 (epub)
Subjects: LCSH: Emotional intelligence.
Classification: LCC BF576 .H65 2021 (print) | LCC BF576 (ebook) | DDC 152.4—dc23
LC record available at https://lccn.loc.gov/2021009971
LC ebook record available at https://lccn.loc.gov/2021009972

10 9 8 7 6 5 4 3 2 1
25 24 23 22 21

Cover design by Rob Watts

Print edition typeset in 10/14 Charter ITC Pro by SPi Global
Printed by Ashford Colour Press Ltd, Gosport

NOTE THAT ANY PAGE CROSS REFERENCES REFER TO THE PRINT EDITION

Dedicated to Austin J. Holder 1937–2020

Father, Friend and Inspiration

'People will often forget the work you have done, they may forget what you have said, although, they will never forget how you made them feel.'

Philip Holder

Contents

Contents

Publisher's acknowledgements

1 Yasmin Dewan: Quoted by Yasmin Dewan; 1 Catherine Robinson: Quoted by Catherine Robinson; 2 Michael Beldoch: Quoted by Catherine Robinson; 51 Denis Burke Sensei: Quoted by Denis Burke Sensei; 66 KamaDeva Yoga: KamaDeva Yoga; 77 Mark Williams: Quoted by Mark Williams, Oxford Mindfulness Centre; 128 Penguin Random House LLC: Roach, G. M., & McNally, L. C. (2009). The Diamond Cutter. New York: Doubleday Religion; 132 University of Vigo: Nakamura, J., & Csikszentmihalyi, M. (2002). The concept of flow. In C. R. Snyder & S. J. Lopez (Eds.), Handbook of positive psychology (p. 89–105). Oxford University Press; 157 and 173 Robert Dilts: Logical Levels of Change model created by Robert Dilts.

About the author

For more than 25 years, I have been inspiring delegates across the globe by assisting them in understanding and developing their emotional intelligence. I have helped them to improve the quality of the impact they have on their own and other peoples' lives.

This book follows many years of empirical study within the field of behavioural science and neuro-emotional intelligence. I have combined aspects from neurology and sociology with elements of business and organisational learning, executive coaching, training, neuro-linguistic programming (NLP), and even from the more contemplative parts of my life using martial arts like Aikido and Tai Chi!

I have drawn much of my knowledge and the techniques I share from working with experts, or senior influencers, across the broad sectors of industry and commerce, social and business networks, as well as from professors, master practitioners and teachers from across an even bigger pool of specialisms.

Many influencers have helped nurture my emotional intelligence, far too many for me to detail here, yet all of whom I am indebted to for the input and support they have afforded me throughout the years.

Following extensive research with more than 700 global leaders in 2006, I developed an emotional assessment methodology which helped to identify the critical elements of emotional intelligence found principally in people who demonstrated exceptional leadership capability.

Several global businesses later adopted this new methodology as a way of identifying and then further developing their future leaders. I have based my writing on many of these initial concepts.

However, the Personal Emotional Intelligence Profile (PEIP) assessment that I have included in this book forms a far broader spectrum of activities and interactions outside of the functions of just leadership and management, making it relevant to everyone, irrespective of their roles in life.

I have personally tested and proved each of the concepts detailed in this book, as I have been privileged to deliver this material internationally through over 1,500 unique workshops, which have, in turn, directly impacted more than 30,000 people.

Following my workshops, delegates have reported a significantly enriched understanding of themselves. They have noticed how improved communication has led to creating far less ambiguity surrounding their behaviours, as well as enabling them to provide clear and concise direction for others to follow.

Discovering your emotional intelligence is not a magic pill that will instantly change your life. I firmly believe that, like all developmental processes, it requires participation and ongoing regular practice.

Foreword

In 2016, the World Economic Forum forecast that emotional intelligence (EI) would be one of the top 10 skills employees would need in the future workplace. That forecast was based on the then growing interest in EI by both business commentators and academics.

Since then, an ever-increasing body of research has provided robust evidence for the value of EI, and few people would now deny that the forecast by the World Economic Forum was accurate.

In a world that is now full of more significant uncertainty than at any time since the Second World War, the ability to express and manage our emotions is fundamental to success, and so is our ability to understand and respond appropriately to the emotions of others.

We humans are, almost certainly, the most emotionally regulated creatures on earth. We all can modify emotional reactions and experiences through an internal process of emotional regulation. At times, these skills require effort, and at other times they appear automatic.

It is important to remember, however, that a considerable amount of our brain contributes to that emotional regulation. Emotions also strongly influence physical reactions. They change body chemistry according to whether the emotions are positive or negative.

We can work to improve our EI by taking advantage of our brain's own physical ability to change.

From a strict business perspective, managing emotions may appear trivial and a 'touchy-feely' soft skill divorced from reality. However, businesses are built on people and, if people can communicate effectively, relate to each other positively, manage change successfully and collaborate willingly, they are more likely to succeed.

The foundation to building EI is a sense of emotional awareness, of being smart about what we feel. Scientists refer to this as 'meta-mood' – a term for a person's reflective, introspective mental experience of their ongoing mood states, such as sorrow, anger, joy or embarrassment.

For those who do not find academic texts the most stimulating way to learn, this book by Philip Holder will be a very welcome opportunity to grasp the theory and importance of EI.

Now, at a time when the world is in a period of unprecedented upheaval and anxiety, the need for emotional intelligence has never been greater. There are many models of EI available in the marketplace, each one with its own set of characteristics. As a result, the range of choices can appear bewildering to those who are newcomers to the subject.

Fortunately, Philip Holder's book provides readers with an opportunity to use the Personal Emotional Intelligence Profile (PEIP), free of charge. This assessment is essential because understanding our EI characteristics is a significant first step in becoming more aware and in helping us to identify areas for further emotional improvement.

The good news from all of this is that, unlike IQ, EI is highly malleable. As we 'train' our brain by repeatedly and correctly applying new emotionally intelligent behaviours, it builds the pathways necessary to convert those behaviours into habits. As the brain reinforces the use of the new behaviours, the emotional hooks supporting old, counter-productive behaviours diminish. As a result, the brain begins responding to its surroundings with enhanced EI without us even having to think about it.

Emotional intelligence is a skill that goes beyond industries, professions, cultures and situations because it is always applicable. Developing EI is an ongoing journey – a journey that differs from person to person. Nonetheless, this book will help you map a suitable route to follow and will make the journey a rewarding experience.

By Colin T. Wallace, PhD
The Center For Applied Neuroscience, Delaware, USA

part 1

What is emotional intelligence?

Emotional intelligence (EI) defines the emotional thinking process that governs those behaviours that, ultimately, shape our entire personality. EI is, therefore, about what defines us as unique individuals.

EI helps us to decide on what matters; it allows us to turn our intentions into positive action, and it describes how we take control of those often unruly, impulsive or negative feelings which stop us from overcoming many of life's challenges. Our level of ability in identifying, understanding, improving and managing our emotions is what will ultimately enable us to adjust to a far broader range of circumstances, and thereby, be able to adapt our behaviours accordingly to suit each new situation.

Furthermore, increased EI enables us to reduce both internal and external conflict. It helps us to remove those stresses or anxieties, which stop us functioning well as human beings and so enables us to live far more rewarding and potentially more successful lives.

To be ready for whatever is likely to be coming our way, it, therefore, makes sense to develop our EI. This process has to start with improving the relationship we have with ourselves first of all, and then needs to define how we improve the relationships we have with others.

The term Emotional Intelligence was first used in 'The communication of emotional meaning', a paper that was written by Joel Davitz and Professor Michael Beldoch at Columbia University in 1964.

This paper no doubt led to an outline of the 'Sensitivity to emotional expression in three modes of communication', which Michael Beldoch also published in 1964.

Both of these papers were early explorations of the psychology of communication and behaviour in different situations, and no doubt laid the initial foundations for the further study of emotional intelligence.

It was not until 1995 when Science Journalist and Author Daniel Goleman launched his book *Emotional Intelligence: Why it can matter more than IQ* that the term found its way firmly into modern language and then into the contemporary world of business.

EI is still a relatively new science for something that we have been evolving, as human beings for over 200,000 years. Ergo it is still likely to continue to be a work in progress as we begin to uncover more and more of what makes us uniquely human.

How to use this book

I have deliberately created the content within this book to be informative and practical as I have used an *experiential* approach, which means that there is plenty of you doing 'stuff', as well as reading and thinking about the subjects we cover.

To get the most out of this book, you will need to take your time as you go through each chapter. Try not to rush through it all in one go and miss completing any of the activities!

I have deliberately used (and not used) certain words, as I am sure you will find out within the text. I have also used positive language structures as well as specific emotionally-intelligent phrases, which I have included because I know from experience just how powerfully they stimulate a whole variety of new emotions and feelings within us.

It is highly likely that, as you go about your everyday life while reading or even after you have read this book, that you will encounter moments of profound realisation. When you do, make sure that you make a note of them, enabling you to reflect and consider more about the incredible journey that you are on.

The book is in two parts; the first provides an overview of what emotional intelligence is and then combines this with *your Personal Emotional Intelligence Profile (PEIP)* assessment.

Unlike any other emotional intelligence test, the PEIP goes a lot further than just reviewing the five dimensions that were previously associated with EI. Instead, it examines our current capacity across 14 different dimensions, defined through 42 elements, all individually measured across 6 levels of emotional efficacy.

In the second part of the book, I have detailed the specific improvements that you can make to improve your level of EI across each one of the 14 dimensions covered in the PEIP.

To ensure that you get the most out of this book, in each chapter, I have included plenty of activities, new techniques for you to try, different approaches and even different ways of thinking about each topic. There are also many practical, real-life examples through the chapters that deliberately underscore the techniques we cover.

Irrespective of your current level of ability, you will, undoubtedly, find some new learning. So, I heartily encourage you to persevere, even if the topic area is not something that you are at first interested in, or possibly it is an area in which you feel you are already adequately capable.

As a result of these activities, I guarantee that you will improve your emotional intelligence. You will gain more confidence; you will become more engaging; there will be less stress in your life, and you will be having a lot more fun.

Plus, you will, inevitably, be improving your overall personal brand at home and work.

Enjoy!

chapter 1

Understanding intelligence

The difference between intellect and emotional intelligence

Emotional intelligence (EI) relates to the part of the brain through which we emotionally connect to make sense of thinking and acquiring knowledge; it further describes our capacity to recognise and understand our emotions as well as to comprehend the feelings and emotions of others.

EQ is very often misused to describe the functionality of emotional intelligence because it relates to emotional 'quotient', which, as the name implies, is a test that ideally should use a quotient scoring method. EQ, therefore, should only relate to a test score and not the level of emotional intelligence a person has as this is likely to become misleading.

When Daniel Goleman first coined *emotional intelligence* in his book of the same name, it considered attitudes across only five dimensions, namely: self-awareness, self-regulation, motivation, empathy and social skills.

As the science around emotional intelligence has evolved and matured, I have deliberately expanded these attitudes further to encompass a far broader spectrum of emotionally dynamic elements that include: *self-mastery, disposition, self-management, influence, stakeholder relationships, developing others, empathy, credibility, communications, team dynamics, leadership, change, collaboration and innovation,* all of which we shall cover chapter by chapter in this book.

By comparison, *intellect* relates to the cognitive reasoning and decision-making processes, through which we know and understand something, and is located in the part of our brain called the cerebral cortex.

IQ relates to an abbreviation of *intelligence quotient,* first used by German psychologist William Stern in 1912 in his book *The Psychological Methods of Testing Intelligence,* which described a scoring method for an intelligence test called *'Intelligenzquotient'.*

IQ is a score found by dividing a person's mental age score, obtained by administering a reasoning and problem-solving test, by the person's chronological age. The resulting fraction, or *quotient,* is multiplied by 100 to find their IQ score.

We need both intellectual reasoning ability and emotional intelligence to get by in this world, although, for some of us, we may prefer to rely more on one of these than the other.

I am sure that we all know those highly intellectual people, whose preference towards facts and data make them appear a little distant to us. This type of introversion will usually contribute to making it difficult for them to communicate their ideas effectively, or to help them build strong emotional relationships with others.

Equally, we will know those people whose preference might not be in solving complex problems. Yet, they will go out of their way to engage with us and then offer endless amounts of help to encourage, support and even nurture our capability, possibly even smothering us with their extroversion.

The difference between these two types of people may seem as far removed as chalk and cheese, yet similar neurological processes are going on inside their minds.

To begin to understand any of this, we first need to take a brief look inside our heads and appreciate how our brains may function in different situations and circumstances.

Rest assured that you do not have to be a neuroscientist to understand any of this. I have deliberately kept the science speak to a minimum and have provided plenty of examples as to how certain parts of our brain relate directly to intellect and emotional intelligence.

Emotional intelligence and the brain

The human brain is the control centre for our entire nervous system. It continuously receives signals from the body's primary sensory inputs such as sight, sound, touch, smell and taste. These inputs get translated via the neocortex into signals or thoughts.

Although many of the processes that keep our bodies functioning are not 'thoughts' as such, they are a combination of electrical and chemical impulses delivered via our central nervous and limbic (emotional) systems which provide the stimulus to various muscle groups throughout our bodies.

The cerebrum is the newest frontal part of our brain, in evolutionary terms, and happens to be the most significant part of our modern-day intellectual brain, because it is here that things like perception, imagination, thought, judgement and decision occur.

There is a band of nerve fibres called the *corpus callosum* which links the left and right halves of the brain; its primary role is to enable the two halves of our brain to communicate with each other. Interestingly, the right-hand side of our brain operates the left-hand side of our body and vice versa.

The cerebral cortex is further divided by the *central sulcus*, which separates the front and back parts of our brain and, most conveniently for us, it helps us to describe four separate regions or cortexes.

Based on the research of Dr Iain McGilchrist (Fellow of the Royal College of Psychiatrists and former Research Fellow in Neuroimaging at the Johns Hopkins Hospital in Baltimore), the following images outline a summary of the functions we understand that each of these cortexes serves.

The *front right* cortex examines abstract patterns. It generates and manipulates internal images of complex spatial information to identify trends and to develop evolving needs. It is this area that governs imagination.

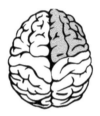

The *right rear* cortex processes harmonic information about relationships, differentiating between tonal qualities or pitches in someone's voice, body positions and various facial expressions, to distinguish between harmonious and discordant relationships.

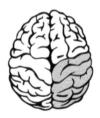

The *front left* cortex examines structures with precision and accuracy, identifying any weaknesses or malfunctions; it evaluates and solves problems to determine if the fault is repairable.

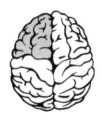

The *left rear* cortex sequentially processes information, it learns and performs a procedure or routine to achieve results, generally involving facts, statistics or objects rather than people.

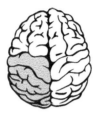

When we consider these cortexes on both left and right sides, we gain a clearer understanding of why we might determine a person as being more right-brained (creative or caring) or left-brained (analytical or processing).

These images also help us to identify how some of these combined functions shape our preferences and, subsequently, inform how we might respond in certain situations.

For example, if we are highly imaginative, like solving problems, although we may dislike order and structure, and possibly are not too worried about relationships, there is a high possibility that we will tend to use more of the frontal two cortexes.

If, however, we prefer people to problems and using creativity rather than statistics (emotions and imagination, to rational and analytical thought), the likelihood is that we will be using more of the two right-side cortexes.

If we are entirely devoid of any creativity, are not too worried about other people and like to get results using a consistent and methodical approach, it is more likely that we have an analytical preference and use the front left cortex.

Do bear in mind that we will also still be using all the other parts of our brain as well; this is more about identifying how our unique *preferences* combine to explain how we behave during work, rest and play.

A fascinating way to help us determine whether another person prefers using more of the right or left part of their brain is to consider which hand is their more predominant when they are communicating with us.

For example, we might notice that a person who prefers being more analytical will tend to use their right hand (if they are right-handed). Particularly, when they are explaining something, we will also see that their gestures are likely to be more focused, succinct or pronounced towards a particular subject or point of view.

They may well be pointing their index finger as they speak or moving a flat hand up and down as they detail specific points. Additionally, their speech patterns will tend towards mirroring their gestures and appear to sound shorter, more concise and a lot more focused.

Whereas, when we are communicating with a person who is using their more creative side, their preference is to use their left hand (if they are right-handed), their gestures will be softer, relaxed, open and a lot more fluid.

Their speech patterns will also reflect this and tend towards using more open, descriptive words, which help them to colour and shape their dialogue.

So, what is the relevance here for being more emotionally intelligent?

The simple answer is that the more we are aware of and understand other peoples' preferences, the more we can adapt our preferences to suit them.

Ensuring that our communication becomes more in tune with their way of thinking, and not necessarily with our own, enables faster understanding of our messages as well as gaining a vital emotional link with them as unique individuals.

A great way of demonstrating this approach is to tune into our communication style and notice our preferences, the pattern of our speech, the type of words we use and the hand we prefer to use when we are talking.

It might, at first, feel a little awkward if we restrict our preferred hand from moving and allow the other hand to operate for us instead. However, what we will undoubtedly discover is that our whole communication style will change and, depending on the situation, quite often for the better!

For example, when I have worked with people to help them improve their presentation skills, I have suggested that they, quite literally, 'swap hands', allowing the opposite hand and the opposite side of their brain (usually the more creative and relationship-orientated part) to take more of an active role in their communication.

You might want to try this out for yourself by simply changing the hand that usually holds a pen while you are talking with another person. I often do this when I am presenting to a large group of people. Ensuring that the open, relationship-orientated and the more engaging side of my brain has preference at that particular time and, more often than not, it completely changes, for the better, the quality of the communication I am having.

This phenomenon might well be the reason why so many weather presenters on television appear always to be positioned to the left of the weather maps, allowing their left hand to gesture towards the weatherboard and not their right. Thus, ensuring that they engage more with their audience rather than appearing to talk directly at or to them.

It might also be why so many politicians appear trained to adjust their hands to more open gestures; rather than allowing their fingers to point at us. Which, by the way, might also remove any perception the audience will form of the politician 'telling' or 'talking at people' when they are being interviewed live on camera!

Before we become too embroiled in the differences between left- and right-handed gestures, we must take note that these may well be opposite for some entirely left-handed people, where the opposite side of the brain will also be affected. In other words, creativity and relationships would be on their left half and analytical and processing on their right half.

I am sure you are getting the idea, so take some time now to think about your preferences and, potentially, the impact that these have on the way you prefer to think and how that influences the way you currently engage with other people.

Activity

Think about which parts of your brain you prefer to use the most and, then, consider how this inhibits or helps you across the many different aspects of your life.
  Some initial questions to get you started:

- How creative are you at work or home, and how does this preference help or hinder you when you are solving problems?

- How comfortably do you relate to new people, and what effect does this have on your work or home life?

- How often might you prefer to keep referring back to facts and information, and what impact does this have on others?

- How comfortable are you at solving complex issues or problems, and how might this preference impact the way you deal with people?

I hope that you are now beginning to understand that it is all down to our personal preferences. And, those preferences relate to the choices we make every day. Unless you have some profound neurological condition, which I doubt, seeing as you are reading this book, you have precisely the same mental capability as anyone else.

Emotional or *intellectual* intelligence is not purely genetic; they both have to evolve through learning and practice. What this fundamental principle means is that it is down to the choices we make that determines the level of our emotional and intellectual intelligence that we use at any particular point in time.

I have outlined, over the next few pages, some of the brain functions that attribute directly to the choices we can make, especially around being emotionally intelligent.

The core of our emotional intelligence

Below the cerebral cortex, we have four distinct areas, which I have outlined in the image below:

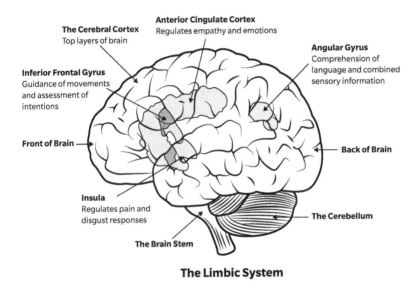

The Limbic System

These areas are within the limbic (emotional) system, located in the central part of our brain, which is involved in interpreting and producing behavioural and/or emotional responses.

Each area plays a significant role in the level of our emotional intelligence and, through adopting the right choices (our preferences), we can increase and, of course, transversely, decrease our level of emotional awareness we choose to have at any particular time.

The *insula* plays a prominent part in filtering the competing feelings of pain and disgust. Interestingly, many different types of people find it challenging to find a balance between these two, often resulting in them having an emotional outburst or even a physical response to something others might have considered to be merely offensive, uncomfortable or inappropriate.

Effectively taking control of the emotions generated by the insula directly affects our responses to other people. For example, rather than choosing to be disgusted, or possibly threatened, by someone's activity, we could choose to become curious about it and engage with that person more effectively to understand their original motivation and purpose.

The *inferior frontal gyrus* is responsible for the guidance of our movements and the assessment of others' intentions. For some people, this part of their limbic system may be overly active, resulting in a requirement for increased personal space. Some people may even appear to back away physically as we move toward them.

Tuning into this part of our emotional brain enables us to choose how we respond to others more effectively in terms of fully understanding their intentions before we react in a way that may be detrimental to effective ongoing communication with them.

The *anterior cingulate cortex*, which regulates empathy and other emotions, is one of the most significant regions that affects our ability to control and monitor our internal feelings. Choosing between good and destructive emotions is what makes us more or less emotionally intelligent at any particular time.

Poor regulation in this part of our brain might result in feelings of insecurity, negativity or self-doubt, as well as our inability to empathise effectively with other people at a superficial or, potentially even, at a deeper level. Whereas good regulation of this part of our brain will enhance our feelings of self-worth, increase our levels of positivity and help us to engender higher degrees of mutual trust or respect and increase our ability to empathise with others.

The *angular gyrus* sits towards the back of the brain. It plays an essential role in helping us to understand auditory language, words, the meaning of those words, as well as the subtlety between the tone and timbre of the language we hear.

It also acts as the interpreter of many of the other sensory stimuli the brain receives; it forms an integral part of our entire ability to learn and communicate.

Choosing for both our internal and external language to be more positive and, thereby, more enabling for others, dramatically improves the relationship we develop with ourselves, and that then increases our ability to create the relationships we have with other people.

Activity

Considering the descriptions above and for each of the following questions, I would like us to imagine a person who might, potentially, have a temporary or a longer-term blockage in one or more of these emotional areas:

1 What do you think would make their communication style different?

2 How might they behave differently from ourselves?

3 How do we think they might struggle at developing relationships?

The answer might well describe a very human genetic or developmental disorder that is shared by millions of people, and that is characterised by our difficulty with some social interaction and by our restricted or even repetitive patterns of thought, communication and behaviour.

We are all 'human beings' after all, whose capacity as an entire species is still in a developmental stage, where some genes dominate in some people more than others, and it is our preferences as to how we use some or all of those genes that make us who we are.

Think of the role that Dustin Hoffman played in the 1988, four times Oscar-winning film *Rain Man*. The portrayal of an autistic savant, being a selective high-functioning individual, who had an extraordinary level of total recall and analytical processing capability, yet found everyday emotional interactions with his brother and other people extremely difficult.

Conversely, we may think about the role that Tom Hanks played in the multi-award-winning, 1994 US epic film *Forrest Gump,* where Hanks played a low-intellect (IQ) man from Alabama, who, through his kind EI-based interactions, witnesses and, unwittingly, influences several defining events that helped shape the USA in the twentieth century.

In all human beings, I sense that there is a constant balance between the forces of intellectual capability and the ever-evolving dynamics of emotional intelligence, even if we may, or may not, have higher levels of intellect.

While some of us overcome many of the genetic deficiencies in our brain by choosing and then adapting to new behaviours, adopting new routines or by using a different range of techniques, none of us is going to be one hundred per cent perfect.

The great news is that, with the right techniques and knowledge, we can significantly improve our EI and, thereby, increase the level of impact we have.

In conclusion, emotional intelligence is not about how much we know, how much we understand or even think we know; it is also not about how fast we can solve problems, discern a wide range of highly sophisticated solutions or even develop a full theoretical hypothesis.

EI sits at the core of our entire being. It is responsible for modelling our personality, our beliefs, the permissions and limitations we set ourselves and, thereby, the impact we have on our lives and the lives of the people with whom we engage.

EI is, therefore, all about how we manage to translate the external world into our inner world and vice versa, shaping how we do things and what we say. It informs the decisions we make in discerning the behaviours for the actions we choose to take.

EI is ultimately about *who* we are and not *what* we are!

Who are you?

I love this question and, whenever I ask it, I always recall it asked of Alice, in the Disney animated film *Alice in Wonderland*. It was asked by the blue caterpillar who, as I remember, for some bizarre reason, was sitting on a giant mushroom smoking a hookah pipe!

In the animation, Alice replies to the caterpillar, 'I hardly know, Sir . . . ' and I think that typifies the answer for most of us. Because we all hardly ever know who we are.

We often prefer to define who we are by our name, sex, nationality, age, role, title or position within a group, family or society situation.

We are rarely able to differentiate ourselves from all the various roles we play throughout the course of our lives.

Although, somewhere behind all of those roles is our 'self', our core being, the inner person who enables our character to come to life in each of the different circumstances we find ourselves.

Activity

Note: you might want to write a few notes at this point, as we shall be using this information again at the end of the book when we look at your unique personal brand and identity.

Give yourself some time before we move on to your Personal Emotional Intelligence Profile (PEIP) assessment to think about *who* you are:

- Be careful not to explain who you are by what you are or what you do. For example, 'I am a female, 29-year-old business analyst' is not what we want here.

- Think more about your human nature by identifying those unique characteristics that you bring to this world.

- Use emotive words that describe your personality, rather than your perceived role in life. Examples might be:

enthusiastic, bold, daring, caring, emotional or unemotional, robust, resilient and maybe, even, engaging.

- You might want to consider the impact that you have on
the people you live and work with and what characteristics
they might use to describe you, such as being introverted or
extraverted, open or closed, positive or negative, warm or
cold, miserable or happy.

chapter 2

Your Personal Emotional Intelligence Profile (PEIP)

Take the assessment

Overview

Now it's time for you to discover your EI profile by taking your PEIP assessment. As part of building your emotional awareness, which is a crucial component of emotional intelligence, we first need to measure and then understand your strengths, together with any weaknesses, across all of the emotions.

The result of the PEIP will give you a clear understanding of your current emotional intelligence levels, so you can better understand your emotional intelligence – your strengths, and all the areas you can improve.

How your PEIP self-assessment works

Following extensive research, I identified six levels of emotional efficacy, which determine how we are most likely to respond across many of the most common dynamic ranges of human interaction and behaviour. These are briefly detailed below:

Level 1: *Against* – when we function against ourselves and others.

Level 2: *Despite* – when we function in spite of others.

Level 3: *With* – when we function along with others.

Level 4: *Harmony* – when we function in harmony with others.

Level 5: *Empowerment* – when we function through empowering others.

Level 6: *Mastery* – when we function at the highest level of EI.

All of these levels are deliberately not restricted to any age or role specifics, making them relevant to everyone, at all stages in our life.

The PEIP assessment scores 42 different elements using these 6 levels as a basis of measurement across 3 sub-categories in each of the 14 emotional intelligence dimensions.

The PEIP, once completed, will provide you with an accurate overview of the *current* level of your emotional intelligence across every one of those 42 elements.

The assessment of your emotional intelligence quite literally needs to reflect the ebb and flow of your life; it is, therefore, best to regard it as a basis for how things are at the moment. In other words, don't think about how you want to be, or what you'd like the answer to be. *Focus on how things are now!*

As your EI develops and your circumstances change, it will be worthwhile coming back to the PEIP to check-in from time to time, so that you measure the progress you are making, or discover what elements will be holding you back when some aspects of your life change.

There are two ways to complete this assessment

Online – this is, by far, the easiest and quickest method. If you have access to the internet, you may prefer to do this assessment online using this link: https://www.philipholder.co.uk/peip. Your full PEIP results and feedback will then be emailed directly to you.

Or

Manually – if you do not have access to the internet or prefer to complete the assessment manually, you can do this by following these instructions – you'll need to add up your scores and do some simple calculations.

Instructions

It would help if you allowed around 30–40 minutes to answer *all* the questions. Although this does not need completing in one go, it is beneficial for you to try and do so if you can. Ideally, finding a quiet space where you can concentrate on your answers without interruption is best.

In each dimension, select only *the sentence that most closely relates to your current preference, and then check the sentence number (in pencil) in the box beside that sentence.*

The accuracy of the results is dependent on the choices you make. Choose only the number that relates closest to the sentence containing your current preference. You must select an answer from each of the 42 elements to gain an accurate result. If you are struggling with a particular response, take some time to think it over and maybe come back to it again.

Then *add* the sentence numbers you have scored together in each of the three sub-categories to find your *dimension score* and then *divide this by three* to find your *average score* across that dimension.

These average scores will enable you to gain the most out of the masterclass section in the second part of this book, as each chapter starts with the six combined aspects pertinent to each of the three sub-categories within it. We will learn more about the six levels in the masterclass section itself.

Important note

You should be aware before reviewing your PEIP that no personal profiling tool, or any other instrument for that matter, that relies solely on self-reporting can be completely accurate.

Ideally, all feedback should be accompanied by a validation process alongside a person who knows you well or a trained professional, whose feedback would involve a good deal of self-discovery facilitated by them using a coaching-based or 'questioning'-styled approach.

Start the assessment

Self-mastery dimension

Self-assessment	Select sentence
I do not assess myself, nor do I make any plans for my self-improvement.	1
I sometimes set unrealistic personal goals and objectives.	2
I assess my capabilities against other people.	3
I regularly set realistic short-term (daily and weekly) goals for my improvement.	4
I create a personal development strategy on a medium-term basis (monthly and yearly).	5
I build a flexible development strategy into my overall life plan; I plan to be successful.	6

Self-confidence	Select sentence
I doubt myself a lot; I generally operate with a lack of self-belief.	1
I sometimes work with a limited level of belief in my skill or capability, trusting that I will get through OK.	2

Self-confidence	Select sentence
I may sometimes appear to be slightly overconfident, or possibly even somewhat arrogant to some people.	3
I am realistic and open about my beliefs and capabilities in most areas.	4
I skilfully balance my beliefs against my capabilities; I always have a high level of confidence.	5
I endeavour to operate daily with confidence in everything I do and demonstrate a positive, yet humble, disposition.	6

Self-control	Select sentence
I often become angry and get frustrated over relatively trivial situations.	1
I am a relatively stable person, although I am sometimes prone to mood swings.	2
People say that I display an air of external calm in most tense situations, although I might appear possibly withdrawn.	3
I am a calm person; I naturally show both inner and outer calmness. I am rarely upset, moody or irrational.	4
I project an air of total calmness. People are calm in my presence, irrespective of the intensity of the situation.	5
I feel at one with myself; I am never flustered and always positive (internally and externally), irrespective of how difficult my life happens to be at any time.	6

Your self-mastery dimension totals	
Add the sentence numbers together to get the dimension score:	
Divide dimension score by three (÷ 3) = dimension average:	

Disposition dimension

Emotional awareness	Select sentence
I do not believe that emotions are essential to a productive life.	1
I acknowledge that sometimes my emotions can influence others.	2
I have a high level of self-esteem; I know my capabilities and the value I bring to other people.	3
I recognise that what I feel is very often portrayed by my demeanour, my actions and my words.	4
I have learnt to identify and accept the feelings that I have and understand the impact they may have on others.	5
I quickly tune into both mine and others' emotional state to ensure the most appropriate communication.	6

Trustworthiness	Select sentence
I sometimes find it difficult to trust people.	1
People seem to be comfortable communicating with me even when I am not entirely sure about them.	2
I trust others only when I am sure that I have reduced all the risks so that it does not create any issues later.	3
I trust that people will do what they say they will do most of the time, although I still need to check to make sure that they are on track.	4
I empower people daily to make decisions about their work and support them only when they have issues.	5
I believe that trust is central to all relationships; I trust all those around me entirely, providing advice and guidance only when required.	6

Conscientiousness	Select sentence
I never take on additional tasks that are outside my comfort zone, role or responsibilities.	1
I sometimes take on additional tasks to assist others, although I do expect the favour to be returned.	2
I like to help people out, although sometimes this is detrimental to my work or time.	3
I am mindful of others; I think about the impact of all my actions towards them.	4
I often go above and beyond to help people get the task completed.	5
I take great pride and care across each aspect of my relationships at work and at home.	6

Your disposition dimension totals	
Add the sentence numbers together to get the dimension score:	
Divide dimension score by three (÷ 3) = dimension average:	

Self-management dimension

Drive	Select sentence
I find it challenging to get started on some tasks.	1
I rarely manage to prioritise tasks daily.	2
I approach every task with the same level of enthusiasm.	3
Each day I have a to-do list that I ensure is completed before the next day.	4
I set achievable goals and objectives for myself and others.	5
I am driven to succeed in every aspect of my life.	6

Commitment	Select sentence
I am not dedicated to anyone or anything.	1
I am committed only to what needs to get done at the time.	2
I am dedicated to the people I support.	3
I easily balance my commitments between people and tasks.	4
I am committed to all who depend on me.	5
I am always entirely committed to all people and all tasks.	6

Optimism	Select sentence
People say that I have a pessimistic attitude.	1
I can be negative in some situations, although I do try to be mostly positive.	2
I am always positive for myself and only sometimes cynical about others.	3
I might be negative for myself, although I am always positive for others.	4
I am optimistic for myself and others.	5
I coach others to be more positive.	6

Your self-management dimension totals	
Add the sentence numbers together to get the dimension score:	
Divide dimension score by three (÷ 3) = dimension average:	

Influence dimension

Motivation	Select sentence
Day to day, I tend to lack motivation.	1
I am mostly motivated by other people.	2

Motivation	Select sentence
I tend to be motivated by status or money.	3
I am motivated in support of others.	4
I am excited by the success of others.	5
I am always motivated, irrespective of any adversity.	6

Leveraging diversity	Select sentence
I am not entirely aware of the individual differences of people (e.g. race, gender, age, ethnicity, physical capabilities or disabilities, sexual orientation, religion).	1
I modify some of my communication and behaviours to suit individual differences.	2
I treat all individuals with respect, regardless of individual differences.	3
I encourage collaborative and mutually beneficial working relationships with people, irrespective of their differences.	4
I comfortably manage individual differences (e.g. resolving conflict, building teams).	5
I foster an environment of inclusion, where diverse thoughts are freely shared, respected and integrated.	6

Political awareness	Select sentence
I do not understand organisational politics, in either a business or social context.	1
I understand that some people have more influence than others in different situations.	2
I recognise the way things need to be done around here to ensure success in most cases.	3

Political awareness	Select sentence
I feel that political savvy is crucial whether liaising with close colleagues, those from other departments, clients or other external contacts.	4
I achieve a win/win result for everyone involved in most situations.	5
I model all the behaviours that consistently bring about success across all environments.	6

Your influence dimension totals	
Add the sentence numbers together to get the dimension score:	
Divide dimension score by three (÷ 3) = dimension average:	

Stakeholder relationships dimension

(N.B. a stakeholder is anyone who is directly affected by what you do; these will be people at home as well as those at work.)

Stakeholder perception	Select sentence
I do not have a distinct understanding of each of my stakeholders' requirements.	1
I assume that I have some knowledge of different stakeholders' needs.	2
I think that each of my stakeholders has separate wants and needs.	3
I understand each of my stakeholders' needs well.	4
I assess my stakeholders' requirements using a wide range of different information and inputs.	5
I have a deep comprehension of every stakeholder's individual, specific or unique needs and wants.	6

Stakeholder orientation	Select sentence
I have a limited understanding of who my stakeholders are.	1
I have a good understanding of who my stakeholders are.	2
I currently focus on my to-do list more than on my how I should 'be' list.	3
I effectively 'tune in' to my stakeholders and adapt my behaviours accordingly.	4
I demonstrate strong social responsibility by including the interests and opinions of every stakeholder in my decisions.	5
I have developed an ongoing, stakeholder improvement strategy.	6

Stakeholder engagement	Select sentence
I have limited or no engagement with stakeholders.	1
I find it challenging to empathise with some stakeholders.	2
I gain a broad perspective of stakeholders' actual versus perceived requirements.	3
I often put myself in stakeholders' shoes to fully understand their issues.	4
I ensure that stakeholders have the chance to define any decision-making process.	5
I consistently build joined-up plans and instigate new initiatives that serve stakeholder requirements.	6

Your stakeholder relationship dimension totals	
Add the sentence numbers together to get the dimension score:	
Divide dimension score by three (÷ 3) = dimension average:	

Developing others dimension

Understanding others	Select sentence
I find it difficult to comprehend some people fully.	1
I sometimes tend to speak over other people.	2
I prefer to listen to other people before I say anything.	3
I tend to say, 'I want to speak with you,' rather than say, 'I want to speak to you.'	4
I like to provide solutions to people's problems.	5
I consult with people, asking open-ended questions and then work with them to achieve joint solutions.	6

Developing individuals	Select sentence
I am not comfortable developing other people.	1
I like to instruct people, telling them what they should be doing in each situation.	2
I enjoy supporting people's development.	3
I often guide and help shape others' capability.	4
I enjoy stretching people's thinking by giving them tasks that help them grow.	5
I fully 'empower' everyone to reach their full potential.	6

Coaching skills	Select sentence
I am not comfortable coaching others.	1
Depending on the situation, I like to provide some guidance to help people out.	2
Although I am not a coach, I do like to help people to grow their skills and capability.	3

Coaching skills	Select sentence
I believe that coaching helps people find their own solutions.	4
I consistently use powerful questions to facilitate others' learning.	5
I am an experienced coach who expertly guides others in making the right choices for their development.	6

Your developing others dimension totals	
Add the sentence numbers together to get the dimension score:	
Divide dimension score by three (÷ 3) = dimension average:	

Empathy dimension

Respect	Select sentence
I do not feel that I can respect everyone.	1
I firmly believe that respect 'must be earned'.	2
I acknowledge that some people are better than me at some things.	3
I place considerable value on other people's ability.	4
I believe that if you show respect, you will get it back.	5
I feel very humble when working with amazing people.	6

Rapport	Select sentence
I struggle to build rapport with people.	1
I find it hard to make eye contact with some people.	2
I am comfortable making eye contact with all people.	3

Rapport	Select sentence
I often match body language or posture with some people, even without thinking about it.	4
I deliberately match body language, tone of voice and pitch with the other person to ensure that we are in sync.	5
I am very intuitive with people, often having a 'sixth sense' about them.	6

Adaptive behaviour	Select sentence
I do not believe in changing my behaviour to suit others.	1
I will adjust some of my behaviour to better associate with others.	2
I consistently demonstrate compassion and support towards others.	3
I flex my communication style to suit different groups, personalities and circumstances.	4
I flex my behaviours as well as my communication to suit different people.	5
I am just like a chameleon: drop me into any situation and I will very quickly adapt to fit in.	6

Your empathy dimension totals	
Add the sentence numbers together to get the dimension score:	
Divide dimension score by three (÷ 3) = dimension average:	

Credibility dimension

Integrity	Select sentence
I do not have particularly strong moral principles.	1
I think it is challenging to have integrity in some situations.	2

Integrity	Select sentence
I believe that you must have integrity in all situations.	3
I pursue a higher level of integrity across my relationships and my work.	4
I am honest with myself and with others.	5
I am entirely dependable to all who rely on me.	6

Capability	Select sentence
I often feel that I lack specific skills or might have a limited ability in some areas.	1
I believe that I can demonstrate an adequate level of capability for my role.	2
I think that, for some things, I have an above-average capability.	3
I am good at what I do and enjoy sharing my ability with others.	4
I consider that I am a consummate professional in my given field of expertise.	5
I am a highly capable person, yet I endeavour to maintain a humble approach.	6

Knowledge	Select Sentence
I sometimes feel that I lack the knowledge required to fulfil my role.	1
At times, I do not make the best use of my knowledge.	2
I believe that knowledge is the most critical aspect of any role.	3
I like to pursue both theoretical and practical knowledge and use that to improve myself and others.	4

Knowledge	Select Sentence
I have a very high level of curiosity about almost any subject or situation.	5
I am a subject matter expert and feel comfortable sharing my knowledge with others.	6

Your credibility dimension totals	
Add the sentence numbers together to get the dimension score:	
Divide dimension score by three (÷ 3) = dimension average:	

Communication dimension

Style	Select sentence
People pretty much must take me as I am.	1
I tend not to adapt or change my communication style – what you see is what you get.	2
I sometimes change what I communicate when in different situations.	3
I often adapt what I communicate to meet the needs of the listener.	4
I always adapt my communication style to suit the situation and the people involved.	5
I can fit in almost anywhere without losing my own identity.	6

Listening	Select sentence
I am quite often accused of not listening.	1
I listen to the things that are essential to me.	2

Listening	Select sentence
My mind sometimes wanders onto something else, and I can miss some information.	3
I am present in most conversations, and I pick up most of the information.	4
I show active listening skills by giving the speaker feedback (replaying what I have heard or asking questions).	5
I easily recall every single aspect of a conversation.	6

Questioning	Select sentence
I tend not to ask many questions.	1
I prefer to use closed questions to keep the answers to concise yes or no answers.	2
I like to ask open questions to gain a deeper level of understanding (e.g. using: who, what, when, where, how, why).	3
I often ask more open questions based on the answers I have just received to draw out the discussion.	4
I use a good mixture of open and closed questions to explore all options and gain agreement.	5
I expertly use questioning to help all parties explore new perspectives and potential opportunities.	6

Your communication dimension totals	
Add the sentence numbers together to get the dimension score:	
Divide dimension score by three (÷ 3) = dimension average:	

Team dimension

Team builder	Select sentence
I am not part of a team; personally, professionally or socially.	1
I provide support for members of my team daily.	2
Although I am responsible for a team, they are all remote.	3
I like to create harmony within the team.	4
I work to enhance team ethos, behaviours and capability.	5
I create a synergistic 'team' approach working towards shared goals.	6

Influencing	Select sentence
I am not good at influencing people.	1
I influence people when I want them to understand my point of view.	2
I quite often use influencing skills just to close other people's objections.	3
I like to ensure that all parties achieve a win/win outcome.	4
I build joint outcomes by taking on-board objections and re-aligning my thought process.	5
I love to create joined-up, compelling outcomes for all parties.	6

Conflict resolution	Select sentence
I prefer to walk away rather than get into conflict with someone.	1
I am not very good at dealing with conflict; I often come out worse than the other person.	2

Conflict resolution	Select sentence
I appreciate that conflict is inevitable and needs resolution.	3
I believe that conflict is an excellent way to bring issues forward and stop them festering.	4
I enable people to find joint solutions to remove conflict.	5
I am a skilled mediator across many different conflict situations.	6

Your team dimension totals	
Add the sentence numbers together to get the dimension score:	
Divide dimension score by three (÷ 3) = dimension average:	

Leadership dimension

Intuition	Select sentence
I find it challenging to read and understand some people.	1
I am not always aware of other people's intentions.	2
I have a good gut feel for most situations.	3
I quickly pick up on non-verbal clues.	4
I very easily pick up on everyone's emotions.	5
I am highly intuitive; I have total awareness of people and situations.	6

Inspiration	Select sentence
I do not believe that I inspire anyone.	1
I think that I inspire some people, although not others.	2
People seem comfortable in following my lead.	3

Inspiration	Select sentence
I encourage some people to develop and grow.	4
I consistently make plans about how I develop my people.	5
People very often say that I am an inspiration to them.	6

Adaptability	Select sentence
I am not comfortable adapting to different situations.	1
I will sometimes adapt how I manage once I can see the benefits.	2
I will always adjust my leadership style if there is a benefit to the broader team.	3
I quickly and easily adapt to how I manage people in new situations.	4
I adjust my leadership style for the benefit of others.	5
I adapt quickly and effectively to changing conditions and flex my leadership style to suit the needs of the people in my team.	6

Your leadership dimension totals	
Add the sentence numbers together to get the dimension score:	
Divide dimension score by three (÷ 3) = dimension average:	

Change catalyst dimension

Instigator	Select sentence
I prefer to leave change to someone else.	1
I like to embark on new initiatives, only when I can see what benefits are in it for me.	2

Instigator	Select sentence
I think that I am resourceful and enjoy coming up with new ways of working.	3
I like to adapt the process and systems to help bring about useful and positive change.	4
I enjoy challenging and changing how 'we do things around here'.	5
I believe that change is constant, and I willingly bring it about.	6

Supporter	Select sentence
I find it difficult to support others during a change process.	1
I endeavour to help others through the change process.	2
I work tirelessly to support new changes, even if I do not entirely agree with them.	3
I support people through change as I fully understand the issues it creates.	4
I encourage others to manage through a period of change using a range of different skills and techniques.	5
I build detailed plans that support others effectively through each part of a change process.	6

Agent	Select sentence
I disagree that all changes are necessary.	1
I agree with change if there is a direct benefit to what I do.	2
Change is constant; if people do not like it, they should leave.	3

Agent	Select sentence
I like being part of the change process if it is not changing for change's sake.	4
I believe that change is the only way of improving.	5
Bring on the next change and let us make it happen!	6

Your change catalyst dimension totals	
Add the sentence numbers together to get the dimension score:	
Divide dimension score by three (÷ 3) = dimension average:	

Collaboration dimension

Networking	Select sentence
I have only a small network of 10 to 20 people that I know.	1
I have a LinkedIn profile only because it is an excellent way to market myself.	2
I have a big network within my organisation, although only a small external network.	3
I have an average network of around 100 people external to my business that I know quite well.	4
I have extensive internal and external networks, which I use to develop my knowledge and capability.	5
I have a vast global network (over 2,000 people) who support each other.	6

Group-working	Select sentence
I am not part of any group; personally, professionally or socially.	1
Even though I am part of a team, because of the roles we work mostly on our own.	2

Group-working	Select sentence
Our team is just a functional silo; it only meets to discuss issues.	3
I work within a team that meets to share knowledge and capability.	4
I work within a fun and vibrant team that both challenges and supports its members.	5
Our team forms part of a much more extensive organisational support network.	6

Long-term relationships	Select sentence
I do not have any long-term personal relationships.	1
I have a few close colleagues and friends, and we keep in touch from time to time.	2
I guess I have an average amount of long-term relationships with people I know well.	3
I have a relatively large number of long-term relationships, some of which are colleagues who I have known for more than a decade.	4
Over the years, many of my clients and work colleagues have become close friends and are part of my network.	5
I have built many long-term relationships with people from across the world, we stay in touch and I very often introduce them to other people within my network.	6

Your collaboration dimension totals	
Add the sentence numbers together to get the dimension score:	
Divide dimension score by three (÷ 3) = dimension average:	

Innovation and creativity dimension

Resourcefulness	Select sentence
I am unimaginative.	1
Sometimes, I find it challenging to think outside of the situation.	2
I tend to use only the resources I have available to hand at any time.	3
I like to find new resources that can support me as I create.	4
I bring together different or unusual resources to enhance the creative process.	5
If I can't find the resource I need, I will create it.	6

Initiative	Select sentence
I often find it challenging to start a new project.	1
I can come up with new ideas, and then I find it hard to put them into practice.	2
I enjoy collaborating/co-creating with others to kick-start a new project.	3
I am the person who always wants to get things moving.	4
I am enterprising when it comes to bringing new projects to the table.	5
I provide a dynamic framework to support new initiatives and ideas.	6

Spontaneity	Select sentence
I tend to be quite contrary and use words like 'no' or 'no, but'.	1
I can be sceptical and will often say 'yes, but'.	2

Spontaneity	Select sentence
I give people the benefit of my doubt and tend to say 'yes, maybe'.	3
I like to be positive and will mostly say 'yes and'.	4
I believe in supporting others and will generally say 'yes and let's'.	5
I am always positive and, often, I will say just 'yes'.	6

Your innovation and creativity dimension totals	
Add the sentence numbers together to get the dimension score:	
Divide dimension score by three (÷ 3) = dimension average:	

Results and scoring

Irrespective of whether you did your PEIP assessment online or manually, the dimension feedback relevant to you will be the same.

Please note: if doing this manually, you may need to round up/down to the nearest whole number if your total dimension score was not easily divisible by 3.

For example: if your three-element scores for self-mastery were $1 + 4 + 6 ÷ 3 = 3.666$, you would round the average *up* to 4 and if, on the other hand, your three-element scores were $1 + 3 + 3 ÷ 3 = 2.333$, you would round your average *down* to 2.

Transfer your average *dimension scores* for each dimension onto the following table and then join the dots together to help you understand the impact of your emotional intelligence across each of the 14 PEIP dimensions.

Level	1	2	3	4	5	6
Self-mastery	O	O	O	O	O	O
Disposition	O	O	O	O	O	O
Self-management	O	O	O	O	O	O
Influence	O	O	O	O	O	O
Stakeholder relationship	O	O	O	O	O	O
Developing others	O	O	O	O	O	O
Empathy	O	O	O	O	O	O
Credibility	O	O	O	O	O	O
Communication	O	O	O	O	O	O
Team	O	O	O	O	O	O
Leadership	O	O	O	O	O	O
Change catalyst	O	O	O	O	O	O
Collaboration	O	O	O	O	O	O
Innovation and creativity	O	O	O	O	O	O

You can now use these scores as a reference point to help you focus on the specific development for each element across the EI masterclass chapters in the second part of this book.

part 2

___

Your emotional intelligence masterclass

The six levels of emotional efficacy

Here is a more in-depth overview of the six levels I referred to earlier and that I have used as the basis to create the PEIP assessment and the book itself.

Level 1: Against

When we are working at level 1, we become far more self-focused or 'I' centric.

We are likely to be very pessimistic and working against other people's thoughts, words and actions, which means that we become less likely to tune in to what other people might be saying or doing.

We may, inadvertently, end up competing with them through the use of either conscious or subconscious dialogue and tend to use very negative language patterns, which are likely to include the use of words such as '*no, but*' at the beginning, or within sentences.

Level 2: Despite

When we are working at level 2, we may appear to be more 'you' centric and, thereby, pessimistically focused towards the other person. We will be more inclined to use a command-and-control approach or a 'telling' style.

The language that we are most likely to have within our conscious or subconscious dialogue will include '*yes, but*', as well as other negative words, such as '*can't*', '*shan't*', '*won't*' or '*don't*'.

Level 3: With

When we work at level 3, we are becoming more optimistic and 'we' centric and, thereby, more focused on positive conjoined efforts and results.

The language that we are most likely to have within our conscious or subconscious dialogue will include '*Yes, and*'. It will also include helpful phrases and questions, such as '*How might we do this?*'

Level 4: Harmony

When we are working at level 4, we are demonstrating an increased optimistic and harmonistic or joined-up approach, which has become a lot more 'us' centric. It engenders the use of everyone's capability and increases the likelihood of a team's success.

The language that we are most likely to have within our conscious or subconscious dialogue at this level will include words and phrases based around the group, such as '*Yes, and let's make this happen*'.

Level 5: Empowerment

When we work at level 5, we are demonstrating a level of optimism and trust that moves beyond team harmony. We are encouraging others to take responsibility for their efforts. Our role is more hands-off than hands-on, we encourage learning through trial and error, failure and success, and our purpose is to help guide and shape their possibilities, not our own.

The language that we are most likely to have within our conscious or subconscious dialogue at this level will include open positively phrased questions using *'Who?' 'What?' 'When?' 'Where?' 'How?'* and even *'Why?'* and all of which, importantly, will negate us from providing any of the answers.

Level 6: Mastery

At level six, we only view the world through the eyes of possibility and potential. When we are working at the highest emotional intelligence level, we are demonstrating such a refined level of optimism, trust, empowerment and engagement that it becomes part of our very nature and our way of being.

The language that we are most likely to have within our conscious or subconscious dialogue will, inevitably, include the single word *'Yes'*.

Using your PEIP results

This masterclass is a complete EI self-development process; I will show you dimension by dimension how you can quickly and relatively easily make small tweaks and adjustments that will each lead to an increase in your overall level of emotional intelligence.

Rest assured that many of these improvements will just happen internally, quite naturally while you are reading and, best of all, with hardly any in-depth cognitive thought process involved!

The main reason for this is down to our emotional awareness. Once we become more aware of ourselves and the impact that we potentially have on others, our brains subconsciously, and almost automatically, start to adjust our behaviours accordingly.

I have included an *Activity* following each section, which will encourage you to think, act, apply, or otherwise disseminate that information within your mind and, when required, apply it to your life.

I recommend that you read all the chapters to enable every part of your EI to improve. You can, of course, focus initially on the low-scoring PEIP areas, improve these and then look to develop in the places where you have scored better.

Daily progress is the key here. It is unlikely that you will instantly adopt a whole raft of new behaviours or a fresh way of thinking immediately, which is why I have deliberately laid out this section so you can come back time and again to help your development.

At the beginning of each of the following 14 dimension chapters, you will find an overview, plus the 6 levels of efficacy associated with each EI element.

Important

Use the *average dimension scores* that you gained to guide you in selecting the right level of the feedback relevant to your current EI in that particular dimension and, thereby, to help form the basis of your learning across the three elements outlined in each chapter.

Note: the reason why we have used an *average* scoring basis for each dimension is that, even if only one element is weaker than the other two, it will still have a detrimental effect on the level of the whole dimension itself.

I recommend reading each chapter in full, even if you have a high score in that particular dimension, as this means that you can potentially use this higher capability to make even more improvements that will aid your ongoing development process.

chapter 3

——

Self-mastery

What is it?

The self-mastery dimension forms an integral part of our emotional wellbeing. It is about how we manage ourselves in different situations, and it forms part of the critical elements we use in helping us to identify the peculiar traits that support or limit us from fulfilling our true potential.

The self-mastery dimension covers:

- Self-assessment
- Self-confidence
- Self-control

Your dimension feedback

Use the *average* score that you recorded for this particular PEIP dimension to review the relevant feedback, as detailed by the corresponding levels of 1 to 6 below.

Level 1: Negative – Self-doubt – Emotional instability

You demonstrate a pessimistic and cynical attitude towards yourself and others; you identify only the worst-case scenario in the majority of situations, you doubt your own abilities and often the skills in others, leading to a poor sense of self-worth, which may result in you openly venting your frustration on or with other people.

Level 2: Unrealistic – Limited self-belief – Mood swings

Your sense of yourself is unrealistic; you demonstrate reduced levels of self-belief, which ultimately will limit the use of some or all of your capability. You are prone to doubt yourself in most situations, which subsequently will lead to an overall lack of fulfilment of your real purpose in life.

Level 3: Validation – Overconfident – Withdrawn

Although you need to seek the validation of your capabilities through other people, you might appear withdrawn or indifferent towards them. Your overconfidence will make it challenging, at times, to build real empathy with people or enable you to demonstrate sympathy when they are struggling.

Level 4: Realistic – Open – Calm

You are realistic about your level of self-worth, believing that your openness with other people, combined with a willingness to adapt and learn more, will enable you to remain calm and positive in many situations.

Level 5: Planned – Confident – Serene

You have an optimistic attitude towards yourself and others; you are confident in your self-worth and believe that you can help define the opportunities for the future, which through additional effort and commitment will help in fulfilling your potential.

Level 6: Flexible – Humble – Positive

You demonstrate a high level of self-consciousness, you have 'quiet' confidence in your unique abilities as well as openly acknowledging and seeking to improve any failings that you may also perceive. You consistently look to find opportunities to develop, physically, mentally and spiritually.

Developing your EI in this dimension

Self-assessment

Through self-assessment, we learn to take better control of our emotions effectively, especially when we are in a state of disorganisation or confusion.

Assessing how we are 'being' in those times, in particular, undoubtedly will serve us better than being ignorant of the impact we may, inadvertently, be having on other people.

Self-assessment is about how, when and where we prioritise and then consciously or deliberately choose to use the emotional characteristics we have within us.

Years ago, when I first started to learn the Japanese martial art of *Aikido*, my *Sensei*, Dennis Burke, used to say to me repeatedly, 'Stop doing and start being.'

Note: in Japanese, *Sen* means before or ahead of, and *Sei* means living or being. *Sensei* traditionally translates as teacher and sometimes is used in leadership or, indeed, both situations.

In Japanese, another word *Ikigai* means simply 'a reason for being' or to provide us with a direction in life. Note the similarity between this word and *Aikido*.

I struggled with the concept of *being* and not *doing* for a long while!

That was until I finally understood that what Sensei was talking about was not just doing each movement; it was about becoming an integral part of it, allowing it to flow and integrate with my thoughts, behaviours and the subsequent actions or responses of my opponents.

What I also came to understand a lot later was that *being* is about using each one of my emotional senses. Being present in every situation meant enabling those senses to inform my thoughts, words, behaviours and then my responses.

Whenever I find myself being present in the moment, I am tuning in to what is going on, using all my emotional intelligence. This, unsurprisingly, gives rise to a myriad of unique and powerful insights around other people, often resulting in those people labelling me as being *'highly intuitive'*.

Whether or not what I describe as *being* is, in fact, *intuition*, I feel blessed to have been able to call upon it and use it successfully throughout much of my professional career.

It has provided me with powerful, often highly revealing, insights about where people are in their current state or situation. It has enabled me to identify what is specifically holding them back and, most importantly, it has helped me determine the appropriate steps that they can take to move forward.

I like to think that being present is when we fully appreciate the moment. We feel calm and relaxed. We know what to do and how to do it, without conscious thought or seemingly any additional effort.

To investigate this further, let us consider what psychologists refer to as a *flow state* and, more particularly, in terms of emotional intelligence.

When we are uniquely focused, we are in a state of *flow*; our focus is on whatever has our full attention at that moment.

We are engrossed with the task in hand and without using any conscious decision-making process. We often lose comprehension of time, other people, distractions and, sometimes, even our basic human needs.

According to psychologist Mihály Csíkszentmihályi, who named the *flow state* in 1975, this is because all of our attention is on the *flow state,* and there is no more attention available to be allocated to other areas!

What I believe is that there is considerably more going on within our conscious and subconscious minds, than just the allocation of one's attention!

There is a pronounced hypersensitivity that links the person in the flow state directly with their task.

Their brains are making precise decisions within nanoseconds; reflexes are enhanced, coordination accentuated, the muscle groups that are responsible for each aspect of the task are receiving the impulses from the brain in the right sequences to ensure success.

When a professional athlete or sportsperson experiences a state of flow, their attention focus is on winning, the goal or target, while their subconscious brains are continually adjusting to each changing condition or situation using all of their emotional and rational senses.

I like to paint and, although competent, I am by no means a great artist; the pleasure and the health benefits I gain through total absorption (being in a state of flow) when I am in my studio are significant.

When I paint, I am relaxed; my conscious mind can wander, I often catch myself thinking about all manner of weird, wonderful and strange things, I even manage from time to time to solve a few issues that may have cropped up in my professional or private life.

What has this all got to do with being present and, more significantly, with emotional intelligence? I hear you ask.

The answer is that it has everything to do with emotional intelligence. When we are in a state of flow, we are present in that moment and it is our emotional intelligence that makes sense of all of the different sights, sounds, physical and kinaesthetic feelings presented to us at that particular moment in time.

I firmly believe that the more emotionally intelligent we are, the more effective and, indeed, the more frequent we will be in a state of flow.

I am fortunate to be engaged by companies who pay me to do the type of work that I love to do. Developing leaders and future leaders has been my stock in trade for more than two and a half decades.

When I am working with a group of managers, I am, often, totally in the zone (in a state of flow). At the end of each day, I find it difficult to recall any of the precise details of the things that have taken place, namely the conversations, exercises or activities.

Yet, through ongoing review and feedback, I know that they have all taken place, in the right order and in the right way.

The only way I can describe this sensation when I work is that it feels as though I am running on 'auto-pilot'. I am not consciously thinking about any aspect of what I am doing or even saying from moment to moment.

Consider the time you were driving a car, and you arrived safely at your destination, without remembering any aspect of the journey itself! We have all done this. It is not because we have been driving without due care and proper attention, far from it. We have exercised good judgement, and we have been safe for ourselves and other road users.

What happens inside our brains during these situations is that our subconscious thought processes continue to function all by themselves, just like an auto-pilot system on a boat, continually monitoring and adjusting to the environmental changes that occur second by second.

Thus, leaving our conscious minds free to think through, review or action anything else that may have importance at the time.

In an emergency, the brain marshals all the neurology from both conscious and subconscious elements to provide the actions required to keep us safe. Accidents do happen, though and, invariably, accidents occur through a lack of concentration. So, what is likely to be going on in these situations?

The answer is 'distraction'. When we are distracted by external influences, our subconscious auto-pilot ceases to work in the same way; our conscious mind focuses towards that distraction, and that's when things can start to become a little messy.

Another theory as to why accidents happen can be based on how we learn new skills. Learning takes place within the conscious mind, whereas learnt behaviour is more likely to reside within the subconscious mind.

Incidentally, there is another reason why accidents happen, and that is due to tiredness. Although I think we will leave this subject for another time!

Time to notice

I often like going for a 20-minute walk to clear my head and help me find a different perspective on a problem.

What I have noticed is that, during the first five minutes of my walk, while I am still wrestling with the issue, my head is slightly down, my eyes are looking at the ground just in front of me, and I am only conscious of about ten per cent of the world around me.

Over the next five to ten minutes, I have noticed that, as I begin to find alternative solutions to my problem, my head is slightly higher, my eyes are scanning a wider field of view and I am conscious of up to 50 per cent of the world around me.

In the final five minutes of my walk, as my head is looking higher, I become conscious of considerably more of the world around me. Usually, it is generally at this point that I have found a resolution to my problem and have also considered the best approach to take.

I wonder if this curious characteristic has anything to do with the reason why motorway police drivers in the UK are trained to focus on the furthest point they can see on the road. To enable them to become more conscious of everything in between that point and themselves and thus boost their conscious minds to respond to situations much faster?

What I hope that you will soon start to appreciate is that much of the emotional and conscious states from one area of our lives can be packaged and re-utilised particularly well in another.

Activity

Take a few minutes to consider when you are genuinely present, scanning the horizon as it were, and in a state of flow. It might be when you are working, driving, playing sport, painting, singing, dancing, cleaning the house, watching a movie, doing the dishes, cooking, entertaining, or just walking the dog.

On a separate piece of paper, write all the emotional words that come to mind about being in that state, for example: happy, engaged, optimistic, motivated, carefree, open, driven, excited, focused, aware, etc.

It might help you also to think specifically about:

- what you see or focus on when you are present.
- what sounds you can hear in your environment as well as the sound of your own (inner) or other (external) voices.
- how you are feeling emotionally and physically.

Now, think about the next difficult task you have to complete and consider how you might be able to transition some or all of these emotional or conscious states into that situation to get a better result.

For example: by lifting your head, putting yourself in a brighter situation, changing your focus, listening to your inner voice more or less, when you are trying to solve a complex problem, will enable you to find a range of different perspectives or alternative solutions.

Self-confidence

Confidence guides the permissions and limitations we give ourselves. It creates certainty, and it also creates uncertainty. It regulates our lives, and it governs each one of our actions, thereby making it a vital aspect of our level of EI at any particular moment in time.

Confidence is the single biggest thing that holds people back from achieving across the life they want to lead, whether this is regarding issues standing in front of an audience, sorting out a complicated relationship, or having to do the right thing to help a demanding situation.

When we think of everyday situations where we may not feel very confident, there is a high chance that our emotional intelligence is working overtime to protect us. It is drawing from previous experiences of perhaps failure, or awkwardness, and it is doing its level best to ensure that we do not have a similar outcome.

Our emotional intelligence can create all manner of additional blocks within our subconscious mind. Through those blocks, we often develop inadequate beliefs systems that govern our internal permissions (or limitations) and, subsequently, lead us towards ever more feelings of low self-esteem and lack of personal empowerment.

A dozen-plus years ago, I was sitting in my office at home, struggling to write a paper about 'Confidence'.

After numerous attempts to get started, I was becoming more and more frustrated and, possibly, due to those frustrations becoming ever more verbal. One of my daughters, called Millie, who must have been around 12 years old at the time, came into my office to ask if she could help.

Not expecting any real assistance, I explained to her that I was trying to define what 'confidence' was and that I needed to describe it in a way that would help other people.

Millie said, 'I'll give it some thought,' And, unsurprisingly, she left me to continue with my endeavours.

After just a few minutes of thinking, though, she returned to my office, made herself comfortable and said, 'Daddy, I think that "confidence" is like a set of scales or a see-saw. If we imagine that, on one side, we have "ability" and, on the other side, we have "belief", and when ability and belief are balanced, we get confidence!'

I was possibly a little bewildered by her instant grasp of the subject matter. However, I did manage to ask her, 'What would happen if "ability" was heavier than "belief" and the scales became unbalanced?'

'Yes, of course, it would be unbalanced,' she replied, 'That would mean lack of confidence due to possibly having low self-esteem.'

I digested this concept for a minute or two before replying, 'OK, smart-arse, what would happen if "belief" was heavier than "ability"?'

At which point, Millie got up from the chair, looked me straight in the eyes and said: 'Oh, Daddy, you're just pretending to be dumb, that would be "arrogance", of course!'

She then turned on the balls of her feet and, with an intentionally arrogant flick of her long hair, she sauntered out of my office, laughing.

Well, to say that I was dumbfounded would have been an understatement!

Simple as ABC

Giving all credit where it's due, I now present what I describe as Millie's Scales of Confidence model. Who would ever have thought that one of my children would eventually teach me my ABC?

$$\frac{A \qquad B}{/C\backslash}$$

A = ability, B = belief, C = confidence

To help put this model into context, let's consider a situation where our level of confidence might be blocking our EI from doing its job and thereby effectively helping us.

An example might be when we are about to deliver a presentation or a talk with a large group of people. Our *ability* and internal *belief* systems will be doing one of three things:

1 *Ability and beliefs will be balanced,* enabling our EI to read the room effectively and deliver a confident communication; which, from our audience's perspective, will feel more tailored towards their unique requirements. The result will, most likely, be them finding our presentation meaningful, engaging and valued.

2 *More ability than belief* will give rise to a range of belief-based communication issues; which include embarrassment, nervousness, fidgeting, a weak or unclear voice.

   Not confidently looking at and engaging directly with the audience will also result in them perceiving us as inadequate, ineffective or, possibly, ineffectual because we do not appear to connect directly with them as people nor with their particular requirements.

3 *More belief than ability* stops us from directly engaging with our audience because we will sound and even look arrogant by talking *at* rather than *with* them. This style of communication is potentially overconfident, it is self-focused, meaning that it is more about us than it is about the audience, which will, most often, result in open or private disagreement, irrespective of any real value in our message.

Activity

Using Millie's model (ABC), think about an activity in your life where the scales of confidence are more likely to be unbalanced and consider what is stopping you from truly succeeding in that situation.

- What is stopping you from being confident?
- How robust are your belief systems in this situation?
- How robust are your skills or capability in this situation?

I wonder how many things we all put off in our lives because we do not have the confidence (the ability and, or, the belief) that we can achieve them successfully.

A few years ago, when I had some time on my hands, I decided that I was, finally, after many years putting it off, going to establish a pond at the bottom of my garden. Although, my garden happens to be on the part of a natural chalk hill where the incline is particularly steep!

I considered my reality and went online to research building ponds into chalk hills, and I was amazed at the level of quite detailed knowledge available. I even encountered a website where this chap had built a fully functional *natural 'swimming' pond*.

Now that was a brilliant idea!

I considered my reality again and, after several more days of research, and learning from many experienced people online, I hired a mini digger.

With much additional help, we ended up digging and lining a 50 ft wide by $6^1/_2$ ft deep hole. This also had a flat $2^1/_2$ ft wide by 10 inches deep shelf around the entire perimeter to hold gravel and pond plants that would help filter more than 75,000 litres of rainwater!

With a little self-belief, many trials by error, learning about all manner of new things (like how *not* to turn over a mini-digger again!), several sore muscles, and many bruises, plus being prepared to call on the help of experts as and when needed, we succeeded.

The result, now the pond has settled in, is spectacular. We have crystal clear swimming water plus a myriad of wildlife and beautiful fauna surrounding our swimming pond. We turned a rather dull grass slope into a thing of natural beauty, which has added substantial value to our lives and our home.

Activity

1 Think of a task that you continuously put off because you are not confident that you can achieve it.

2 *Consider your reality.* In other words, is it possible for someone else with a similar level of ability, skill and knowledge to yourself to complete this task?

3 If the answer to 2 is *no*, then you will need to ask yourself *what new skills you could learn* that would enable you to have a go and potentially succeed at this task.

4 If the skills or knowledge are not currently available to you, consider which aspects of the task would get completed with additional help or expertise, and which are those activities that you might cover by stretching yourself.

5 If the answer to 2 is *yes*, then you might need to stop procrastinating, which, incidentally, is more about not believing in yourself or your abilities and putting these to the test, than it is about identifying all the reasons why you should not even have a go.

As you may have guessed, I am a dedicated believer in learning through doing. I also believe that nothing is impossible if you put the effort in up-front. When we think that something is possible, all we need to ask ourself is how we are going to achieve it!

I am not just talking about DIY projects; this way of thinking is useful across all aspects of working and personal life. An excellent method to use when we are trying to *consider our reality* in different situations is to ask, 'What? Why? So what?'

I use these three questions, in this particular order, when I am doing what I call '*instant coaching*', where someone may have reached an impasse in their thinking and is struggling to move on to the next stage.

For example:

- *What* specifically are you looking to achieve?
- *Why* do you want to achieve this?
- So, *what* is holding you back?

And, then, based on their answers, a similar process is repeated:

- *What* things can you alter or change?
- *Why* would that make a difference?
- *So what* actions could you now take?

The sets of what, why and so what questions can be repeated several times, in different formats, until the person has identified for themselves what needs to happen for them to achieve the outcome they require.

I find this tool also very useful when I am struggling with a new concept or a problem. I ask myself three linked questions, each starting with what, why and so what.

The result is often a far deeper clarity around the topic. It is, after all, another way of testing the reality of a situation, issue or problem, and it gets results quickly and effortlessly.

Try it out for yourself with a current problem or use it to enhance the last *Activity* we just covered.

Self-control

A reasonable definition of self-control is the discipline we practice over our emotions, impulses and desires.

On this basis, we should be able to prevent ourselves from acting, reacting to something, or from feeling something that we do or do not want to feel.

Concerning emotional intelligence, self-control is not just about choosing which foods to eat, denying ourselves certain luxuries, or limiting our excesses in anything that may, potentially, be bad for us!

It has far more to do with restraining those attitudes and behaviours that might otherwise inhibit positive outcomes. Anger, stress, anxiety, frustration and even arrogance can often bring a consequential negative impact on what might have been a positive result.

Yet, those emotions can be so powerful that they are difficult to bring under control in the heat of the moment.

We have all been there; where, one moment, everything in the world is going smoothly, only to find that, through a brief lapse in concentration, we have (or someone else has) made a silly error, and our beautiful world suddenly becomes chaotic.

The best approach would be to accept that errors are what makes us human and that through these problems come knowledge and potential learning, which may be all very good in theory. However, in the heat of the moment, it is incredibly tricky to control our reactions.

When I interviewed several hundreds of people in pursuit of learning about higher levels of emotional intelligence, what I discovered was that those people who were already at the top of their game were the ones who managed to successfully 'channel' their negative emotions.

After further research, I also discovered that each of those people managed to 'channel' their emotional state in pretty much the same way, resulting in a vastly improved level of self-control and, as a massive bonus, significantly higher levels of self-confidence.

I first learnt the techniques that I am about to share from my practice in martial arts. Later, I discovered that all the people who were extraordinary at managing self-control, and happened to demonstrate high levels of self-confidence, were, in many cases, subconsciously using precisely the same techniques.

Further research led me to understand that this was by no means just a lucky coincidence. In each case, I found that when people were accessing a 'channelled' emotional state, the same metaphysical and physical responses happened.

Finding your centre

The first of these states is what we will call being 'centred'.

To find our centre physically, we will at first need to stand upright, with our feet slightly apart and in line with our shoulders.

Next with our right hand, held flat on our stomach, with our fingers tight together, we place our index finger over our navel, with the rest of our hand flat and held square on our stomach.

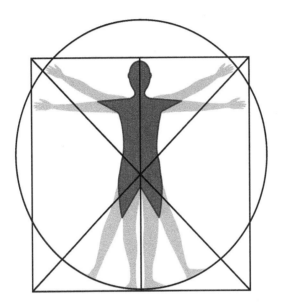

We then draw an imaginary line with our left index finger from the fingernail on our right index finger, down until we find the space at the top of our right little finger.

We remove our right hand altogether, leaving our left index finger pointing directly in towards our lower stomach (approximately two inches below our navel).

Next, we imagine a line coming down from the top of our head through the centre of our body.

We now join that vertical line at right angles with the horizontal line from where our left index finger is pointing, towards our lower back.

That internal point, located in the middle of our lower gut, is where those two lines intersect, and it is our 'centre', or for anyone who practises Yoga or Pilates we might know it as our 'core'.

Incidentally, it is one of the seven Chakra Points called the *Sacral* or *Sacrum* and, in martial arts, it is often called *Tanden* or *Hara*, being the centre of our balance from which all movement comes.

A remarkable thing happens when we focus our attention on our centre: not only do we become mentally balanced; we also become physically very stable.

In an exercise I use when I am running a workshop, I have people work in pairs, where each person stands alongside the other. The first person thinks about a point somewhere around the middle of their forehead.

The second person assists them by placing a hand gently on their shoulder and applying a small amount of lateral pressure in any direction.

The result is that the first person will always move or sway a little as they are both mentally and physically pushed off-balance.

In the second part of the exercise, the first person locates and then focuses their attention around their 'centre', as described above.

When their partner then applies lateral pressure to their shoulder, the result is no movement at all, they have magically become solid and stable.

The results are always the same. Once delegates have located their 'centre', they become more robust, better balanced, and far more in control within their surroundings.

Let us now briefly explore why this phenomenon exists. When we touch or think about a point on our forehead, we are sending a message to our cognitive (reasoning) brain that is determining whether that touch is a threat or something else.

It is just a two-dimension, locational-specific perspective, which momentarily uses a lot of the wrong type of brainpower. Because our attention at that time is on that single external point, we become physically unbalanced, or possibly even top-heavy.

If we watch someone when they are rooted in deep cognitive thought, we will notice that their heads are slightly down, and their posture is somewhat forward of their natural vertical line of balance.

On the other hand, when we focus our attention on our core, we are using a three-dimensional location, which is in the middle of our entire being, it helps us to become aligned with both horizontal and vertical lines of balance. By the way, it also subconsciously raises our heads!

Another interesting fact is that our centre is at the very end of our brain stem, which is linked directly into our limbic system, in the central part of our brain and, as it also just so happens, governs most of our emotional intelligence!

Quite recently, scientists discovered that there is a direct neurological connection between our brain and our gut, with up to a hundred million neurons potentially located in the lower abdomen, providing immediate feedback through our central nervous system to our brain. No wonder we sometimes experience a sinking feeling in our stomach when things are not going right for us.

The more physically centred we become, the more balanced we are both physically and emotionally.

Relaxed

The second state I would like us to think about is the state of being fully relaxed. I do not mean just laying back in our chair here and closing our eyes, type of relaxed. I am talking about becoming physically and emotionally totally relaxed.

Let us start with our breathing. Take a deep breath now and hold it for a few seconds and then breathe out slowly.

Which part of your body moved? Your upper chest and shoulders?

Most of us breathe very badly during our waking hours, we take a breath, and it occupies around only a third of our lung capacity.

Yet, when we are in a deep sleep, we breathe very differently. We take a breath using the muscles around our diaphragm, our chest only expands at the lower part of our abdomen and not further up towards our shoulders – see below.

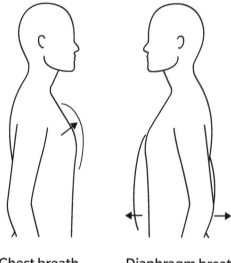

Chest breath   Diaphragm breath

A regular diaphragm breath can double the amount of air we breathe to around 60 per cent more of our lungs' overall capacity. This means that we take in more air, and more air equals more oxygen getting into our blood supply, and thereby more oxygenated blood reaches our brain, which further results in an increase in our brain's metabolism.

Increased brain metabolism relates directly to increased brain power, with fewer breaths, which improves our ability to relax, plus there is considerably less wear and tear on our bodies.

To take a diaphragm breath, try the following: place a hand just below your navel and take a breath. If your hand moves inwards, that is a chest breath; only when your hand moves away from your stomach is that a diaphragm breath.

If you are finding this difficult, try to focus your attention on your 'centre' and breathe deeply and slowly around that point.

Take a few deep breaths and notice the difference. Be careful not to overdo this, to begin with, and, if you are feeling a little giddy, that is just your brain reacting to all that lovely increase in oxygen and those giddy feelings will soon pass.

We all need a few deep diaphragm breaths from time to time to help get us into a pleasant relaxed state, to settle any nerves, remove erroneous emotions or even just to wake ourselves up.

That is, after all, why you are about to, or may already have just, yawned!

Being light

The third state I wanted to discuss is a state of mind and not a physical characteristic. Although with a 'light' state of mind, it might appear to some that physical activity happens with minimal amounts of effort.

If you have ever seen a true master at work in any profession, whether that be a carpenter, musician, or a sportsman, what we notice is how effortlessly they appear to get results.

Although many years of practice, learning and skills development have gone into their craft, they appear to do their work effortlessly, and some might say, even, with a light touch.

As previously discussed in the section 'Self-assessment', when we are 'being' in a state of flow, we are, in essence, 'being light'. Our mind and bodies are elegantly combined so that we become entirely in tune with what we are doing.

There is another more profound physical effect of 'being light', and that is becoming so strong that it is almost impossible to move you. Let me explain this through an example of when I have seen this happen.

Sensei Dennis, whom I mentioned earlier, and I were teaching rugby to children on a Sunday morning at our local rugby club.

Dennis was coaching a much older age group than my seven-to-eight-year-old youngsters. His team were struggling with creating a robust defence.

I watched him ask half a dozen burly teenage youths whom he was coaching to grab hold of him, or bits of his rugby kit, and pick him up off the ground.

The result was an easy enough task that these half dozen youths managed with comparative ease, considering that Dennis is around six feet tall and, through decades of daily physical Aikido practice, solidly built.

I remember him laughing and goading them on to lift him higher. Then, after just a very short pause, when he was standing firmly back on terra firma, he challenged them to repeat the exercise.

The second time around, they just could not pick him up, not even when Dennis encouraged all the members of the squad to get involved and add their strength to the mass of bodies trying to lift what had seemingly become an impossible weight.

There was no magic trick here; it was the combination of mind and body strength and a little-known term for me at the time, which Dennis called 'being light'.

It still amazes me, even now, 20 years further on, how with 1 single technique Dennis empowered a whole group of 20 or so young men to become extraordinary and rarely bettered rugby players. One or two, I believe, went on to become professional players and Dennis himself went on to coach the new fledgling England women's rugby team at that time.

The only other way I can describe this is with one of my daughters, who, when she was three or four years of age, decided that she was not going to bed and laid on the floor, completely relaxing her entire body. She became so heavy through being light that it almost made it impossible for my wife and me to physically pick her up between us and take her upstairs to her bedroom.

When we are mentally 'being light', we become physically stronger. We have all heard incredible tales of heroism, where, against all the odds, a person has managed to overcome physical boundaries, which otherwise would have stopped them.

I remember a story in a newspaper of a young mother who, quite literally, picked up the back of a motor car to pull out a young child who was trapped beneath.

I am sure we will have all heard and read about many similar stories where the impossible becomes possible, through sheer determination and through the application of more physical strength than would appear likely.

I can only hazard a guess as to what is going on inside the minds of these incredible people. There is no simple explanation. Yet, each of these heroes has said the same thing that they were only thinking about what needed to happen and just did it.

They did not concern themselves with how, or why, they were just in the moment, totally focused on what needed to happen and they did it, irrespective of their physical limitations.

'Being light' for me is when I am in a state of flow; I cannot suggest that I become superhuman and my strength doubles. Nor will I recommend that there is an additional benefit to anything other than improved self-performance.

Although, I can attest to having had some of my most rewarding experiences where I have achieved results well beyond my initial capability through adopting a 'being light' state of mind.

Focus

The final state that I attribute to both improved self-control and higher levels of self-confidence is focus.

Focus, likewise, goes hand in hand with being in the state of flow. When we focus entirely on the task in hand and nothing else, we become both mentally and physically absorbed by its completion.

There is an exercise I use in my training workshops to demonstrate this, called 'Unbendable arm' (N.B. you may want to find another person to help you, if you're going to practise this).

Delegates work in pairs. Person A stands upright with their preferred arm resting by their side. They then bend their lower arm up at the elbow to form a right angle with their upper arm, with a clenched fist facing away from them.

Person B then tries, using reasonable care, to bend person A's clenched fist up towards their shoulder.

It only requires a little bit of strength to achieve this, especially if person B is using two hands, where one hand gently grips just behind person A's elbow, and the other hand gently grasps their wrist, thus creating a type of fulcrum point for the movement.

In the second part of the exercise, person A is told to open their hand flat, with the thumb at the top, so that all fingers are straight and pointing away from their body.

Person A then is asked to focus on any external *point of reference*, which could be a window across the street or a tree in the field next door.

The more they focus on whatever it is beyond themself, the stronger they become, so much so that it becomes almost impossible to bend their arm as before.

Delegates often try to find reasons as to why this works. They suggest that there might be a muscular or physical explanation for the significant change.

What I do know, from experience, is that, when we are entirely focused, there does not appear to be much physical effort involved at all!

Activity

Centre – Relax – Being light – Focus: think of a situation when you may be in danger of losing some of your self-control; it might be a situation where you feel tired, fed up, confused, angry, frustrated or even just a little miserable.

1 Find your centre and think about that core expanding within you.

2 Take three or four diaphragmatic breaths, around your core, breathing slowly in and slowly out, filling as much of the lower lung space as possible, each time.

3 Change your mind from letting it become burdened or weighed down with current problems, anxiety, or frustrations to becoming light and fluid. Letting go of the issues you are currently mentally wrestling with may help you to find alternative approaches.

4 Focus your attention 'through and beyond' the problem or situation and onto a new 'point of reference' like a positive outcome.

These same techniques are suitable for all areas of our lives, even when things are going well, and we want to heighten the experience.

As previously mentioned, the same techniques are useful in difficult situations where we may lack the confidence we need to move forward.

These techniques, although more physical in approach, have a profound effect on our thinking modality and help us to effectively re-program how our mind is working at a time of need or even when we are in a state of crisis.

Practise these techniques daily in every situation in which you find yourself and, before too long, you will be amazed at the level of mastery you have achieved.

chapter 4

Enhancing your disposition

What is it?

The disposition dimension relates to those inherent qualities that define our character or the natural way we tend to do things. Our nature thereby determines the perception others have about us, as well as our natural inclination towards certain behaviours or actions.

The disposition dimension covers:

- Emotional awareness
- Trustworthiness
- Conscientiousness

Your dimension feedback

Use the *average* score that you recorded for this particular PEIP dimension to review the relevant feedback, as detailed by the corresponding levels of 1 to 6 below.

Level 1: Unemotional – Untrusting – Unenterprising

You appear to be too laid back and lackadaisical, often demonstrating a lack of enthusiasm or showing any determination to get things done. You will not express your emotions well to others, making it difficult for people to comprehend you entirely, which might lead to them developing negative or unrealistic perceptions about you.

Level 2: Reserved – Mistrusting – Calculated

Your apathetic nature means that you do not always readily demonstrate your feelings; at times, you show limited interest, enthusiasm, or overall concern for other people's wants and needs, which may result in them becoming directly critical of you.

Level 3: Self-esteem – Mitigation – Accommodating

Your casual approach to life demonstrates a high level of self-regard. In contrast, this may negate the opportunity for others to get to know you a little better, as you are likely to find trusting other people difficult at times and, even though you want to assist, you may prefer just to get on and do things by yourself.

Level 4: Demeanour – Trust – Mindful

Your demeanour is one of caring for others, as you are most likely to think carefully about the impact you have, and you appear to be concerned for them. While you understand some of your own emotions, you may not always pick up on other people's feelings, mainly because of your need to check up on them regularly.

Level 5: Feelings – Empowerment – Helpful

You are interested in understanding how your emotions affect other people. You take time to understand others more and feel comfortable entrusting them with tasks that will enable them to develop and grow. You will go out of your way to help and support the people around you.

Level 6: Emotionally aware – Trustworthy – Conscientious

You are highly curious about the relationships you forge; you seek to understand yourself and others at a profound or deep level. You elegantly enable others to perform by empowering them to work at the highest levels of their capability. You demonstrate a diligent and conscientious approach across all aspects of your life.

Developing your EI in this dimension

Emotional awareness

'Emotional awareness is the ability to recognise our own emotions as well as those emotions of the people around us.

Emotions are those incredibly complex feelings that, according to some theories, "are the states that result in physical and psychological changes that influence our behaviours".'

Many people experience what can be referred to as an amygdala hijack when faced with different types of internal or even external conflict, which can then be the cause of fear, anxiety or even stress.

Amygdala hijack is a term coined by Daniel Goleman in his 1996 book *Emotional Intelligence: Why it can matter more than IQ.* There is a whole biological explanation for the amygdala hijack. Stated quite simply, the amygdala hijack equates to 'freaking out' or seriously overreacting to an event.

In everyday situations, we tend to process information through our neocortex, a part of our cognitive 'thinking brain', which is where 'logic' occurs. The neocortex then transmits the information to the amygdala, a small almond-shaped organ that lies deep in the centre of our emotional brain.

On occasion, there is a short circuit whereby the cognitive or thinking brain has been by-passed, and the signals are sent straight to the emotional brain. When this happens, we have an immediate, overwhelming emotional response disproportionate to the actual event itself.

A while later, information relayed to the higher brain regions, that perform logic and decision-making processes, causes us to realise the inappropriateness of our initial, emotional response.

To discover why this happens, we may need to go back in time, by several thousands of years, and consider when an immediate emotional response might have served a different purpose.

Imagine that we were on an expedition to find food for our families and, while we are gathering our supplies, we encounter a giant and very hungry meat-eater!

In such a situation, the brain needs to respond quickly, as it doesn't have time to mess about with logic or rational thinking. The amygdala takes over the brain's functions, it then enables the pituitary gland (at the base of our brain) and the adrenal glands (on top of our kidneys) to release adrenalin throughout our bodies, resulting in what we now term as a *fight or flight* response.

Nowadays, we are far less likely to encounter hungry meat-eating animals when we need to go out to find food. We are, however, almost sure to meet drivers that cut us up on the road and we may even have to deal with other disrespectful people who push in front of us when we are selecting our choice of foods.

What can we do about it?

Knowing about the amygdala hijack allows us to prevent it ourselves by remaining aware of our emotions during potentially triggering events, or to consider that the overwhelming emotional response from someone else might be due to them experiencing an amygdala hijack.

A useful way to prevent amygdala hijacking is to use an eight-second rule. Waiting for just eight seconds causes the brain chemicals that cause amygdala hijacking to diffuse sufficiently.

Breathing deeply from our core and focusing our attention on something pleasant helps prevent the amygdala from commandeering the brain and causing an extreme emotional reaction.

The more emotionally aware we become, the more we are enabled to choose to make those changes that bring about more positive outcomes.

Some people might refer to emotional awareness as 'mindfulness'. Professor Mark Williams, former director of the Oxford Mindfulness Centre, says that 'Mindfulness means knowing what is going on inside and outside ourselves, moment by moment.'

When we have more profound clarity over the present moment, we understand ourselves and the impact we have on our world far better. We can choose to notice even the smallest things, such as quieter sounds, different flavours and smells or the things we touch, like the feeling of a door handle when we enter a room.

Through becoming more aware of each moment during the day and recognising those feelings that are present in that moment, we begin to experience afresh things that we have, so often, been taking for granted. Emotional awareness helps us to enjoy the world around us more, as well as gaining a better understanding of ourselves.

Well-documented research suggests that it significantly contributes to improving our mental wellbeing, which, in turn, often reduces stress and anxiety.

77

I do not believe that just tuning into more of our external sur-roundings is sufficient; emotional awareness is also about tuning into our internal voice.

Listening to all those erroneous thoughts will add a new layer of cognition and, thereby, a far more in-depth understanding of the present moment.

When I am coaching someone with a business problem, I very often have them describe the situation that is causing them concern, in immense detail.

I get them to explain what is going on 'specifically' and then I encourage them to frame all their answers using all their predomi-nant senses. What they feel, what they hear and what they see.

For example, I might ask them: 'How does that make you feel, specifically?' 'What did you hear, precisely?' or 'Describe what that particular scene looked like in more detail.'

Very often, these questions result in that person gaining a different perspective of what is happening in that reality from which they are then able to find an alternative approach or resolution.

There is more to the practice of becoming more mindful than just tuning into our emotions. A mindful approach is to consider every action and, thereby, those reactions that we, or indeed others, may have.

An excellent technique for mastering emotional awareness is meditation. Meditation is a state of overall awareness and, thereby, it helps us to gain a far healthier perspective on all aspects of our lives.

During meditation, we are not trying to turn off or even manage our thoughts and feelings; we are merely observing them without judgement and seeking to understand them further. Some people might also call this process self-enlightenment.

Many people choose to meditate at a specific time of the day; they will find a quiet, comfortable space and start by closing their eyes, breathing in deeply, slowly and deliberately until they begin to feel physically more relaxed.

They might then choose to think about a subject that they wish to concentrate on and, while exercising 'no judgement', they explore all the aspects surrounding it.

There is no right or wrong way to meditate, it is a personal thing and a personal choice. I am sure that you will find many different avenues to explore should you wish to locate further help in getting started.

My personal preference is to practise meditation soon after I awake every morning, while I still lie in bed, allowing all my thoughts to flow and merge without judgement. Sometimes, those thoughts materialise into new creative ideas, solutions, alternative plans and, sometimes, they do not reach any conclusion at all. What is essential is the process, as I can honestly say that I start each day with positive energy and, most importantly, an open mind.

Meditation aims to enable us further to become calmer and more reflective whenever it is required and, thereby, turn any problems into solutions effectively as they each arise.

Meditation, for most of us, is likely to be a work in progress. I am no expert and, just like everyone else, I still fall into the anxiety trap from time to time.

Yet, as I learn to manage each of the feelings and thoughts that might attribute towards my anxiety, I gain better control of the next negative perspective that may be trying to attack or unsettle my conscious thought process.

Activity

I would like you to think of a current problem, situation or an emotional state that is holding you back.

1   Write it down on a piece of paper and look at it.

2   Read aloud what you have written and, at the same time, listen to hear the word or words that you subconsciously emphasise the most (it might be a slight inflexion in your voice, a rise in volume on that word, or a pause before or after saying it).

3   There is a high chance that these emphasised words will relate to your current beliefs (the permissions and limitations we set ourselves) and will likely be causing you an issue.

▶

4   Concentrate on just one of those words at a time.

5   Close your eyes, only if you feel comfortable doing so, and try to see the word written in your mind's eye.

6   Focus your attention 'through and beyond' that word, allowing your mind to wander wherever it needs to go and do not try to control or force it to find answers.

7   Breathe deeply and slowly, with a diaphragm breath, slowly relaxing deeper into a subconscious state.

8   Notice your different thoughts, notice your breathing, notice noticing yourself and allow that process to continue for as long as it takes.

9   When you have opened your eyes (if you had them closed), you may feel considerably more relaxed, maybe even a little more refreshed and revitalised.

10   You may also have resolved the problem or situation, or possibly you will be another step closer towards that end.

11   Repeat steps 1–10, if necessary, choosing a different word to focus on each time.

While doing the above exercise, you will have automatically increased your emotional awareness. You will also have learnt to take the first formative steps in the practice of meditation.

As you progress to practise these techniques more, you will start to uncover a more individual approach and methodology towards stronger self-enlightenment and certainly towards more profound relaxation.

Note: we are not the same; what works well for me may not work for you. You may need to identify a different technique from the one outlined above.

The important thing is that you do 'emotional awareness'. The vehicle you choose to get to it is not the vital thing; only the destination itself is what is essential.

Trustworthiness

I believe that trust is a critical aspect of defining our emotional intelligence in any given context, whether it be individually, collectively, or as whole organisations of people.

We all know just how important that single word 'trust' is. We also know what it feels like when trust is absent. Each word and action is recorded in the subconscious part of the brain. It gives us clues as to the trustworthiness of others.

It is not just what people say and do that creates trust; it is also how they behave, react, move, even breathe. Pretty much every element of human behaviour sends out strong messages about the level of trust we perceive in other people.

Think of the last time you were having a conversation with someone when they did not make direct eye contact with you. How did you feel towards this person, did you trust them?

We all know what it is like when those people we are trying to engage with prefer to look at their mobile phones or computer screens, or somewhere else in the room. When we are talking with them, it can sometimes make us feel uncomfortable.

If this does happen, we need to be mindful of their perspective; have we broken their trust? Are they intimidated by us? Have we said something that may have upset them in some way? Might they be less confident than we are? Or are they just not interested in what we have to say?

Note: please be aware that, in some cultures, direct eye contact relates to impoliteness, or even, to some, as being downright rude.

Although, for most people in the Western part of the world, lack of eye contact usually means that someone is evasive, rude or possibly hiding something deliberately from us.

Just a thought here, have you ever noticed that the people who have high emotional intelligence are also the ones who comfortably make direct eye contact with you and others?

How would we feel about having a meaningful conversation with the chap who is covering the service area at a car dealership, where we go to discuss a problem we are having with our expensive new motorcar?

The chap on service reception is very scruffy, slumped in a chair, with his hands behind his head. He is sitting back, looking at the computer screen in front of him and does not look at us, even when he asks what the problem is.

How much do we trust him at that moment in time to be able to help us solve our problem?

I am sure that we can think of several similar situations where, just through the other person's look, actions or body language, we have not felt that we can entirely trust them, let alone rely on them to solve our problems.

Think of the people who have let us down in the past. Even though they may have convinced us that they will show up, in whatever way promised, they did not. Did they maybe give us some small clues that they might not do what they had said?

It is highly likely that the clues were there in their posture, their voice or even in their actions. Yet, we did not hear them or see them because we were probably not being emotionally intelligent ourselves at that moment.

When we are truly present, we naturally pick up on the other stuff. 'Stuff', by the way, is the plural of 'it', and all of the 'its' are the essential behaviours that we need to be mindful of in others!

Several years ago, I set myself a mission to try and define what trust is and, more importantly, how I could help others to appreciate and develop it. After a considerable amount of research and an awful lot more error than trial, I finally managed to come up with this explanation:

$$\text{Trust} = \frac{\text{Empathy} + \text{Credibility}}{\text{Risk}}$$

Let me explain what this means. I believe that for trust to be present in any relationship, it needs to have the right amount of empathy and the right amount of credibility, depending on the level of risk involved.

In other words, the higher the risk, the more empathy and credibility need to be established!

Let's say that someone we have only recently met wanted to borrow £1 from us, so they could buy a sandwich at lunchtime, with a promise that they would give it back to us tomorrow. Would we consider lending it to them if we had the money on us?

Many people would be OK with this if the person looked as if they could afford to pay it back, and we happened to like them, based on the limited knowledge we have about them and because a single £1 is probably not going to put too much of a hole in our finances.

Now, consider the same person asking to borrow £10 from us. How do we feel now?

What about £100? Or even £1,000? It starts to get considerably harder to say yes, even if we had the money. As the level of risk increases, so does the level of trust!

Consider the same situation for someone we know and completely trust. If we could afford it, how much would we be prepared to lend them?

In the world of commerce, financial institutions spend a great deal of time and effort in managing their risks by ensuring that they have a full picture of the actual credibility of their borrowers and investors.

I wonder, if they were to spend a little more effort on under-standing and developing empathy with their customers, whether some economies might be a bit more robust and a lot more vibrant? Maybe, I should leave that topic for future discussion!

We all make internal judgements on the trustworthiness of others on a day-to-day basis. Yet, we seldom think about how we can become more trustworthy ourselves.

What would happen if we asked ourselves this question: 'If consid-erably more people trusted me, what difference would that make to my life and theirs?'

Maybe, it would make us a better manager or leader; we would perhaps win more deals, possibly more people would seek our advice and guidance, perhaps we would simply become more authentic in our role and our life.

Whatever your answers were, we could all do with being a lot more trusted and, indeed, trusting of others. So, let's dig a little deeper and try to get a better understanding of trust and, more importantly, how to become more trusted.

> **'Empathy is the capacity to understand or feel what another person is experiencing from within their frame of reference, that is the capacity to place oneself in another's situation.'**

We might also think about empathy as the catalyst that enables a relationship to work smoothly and effectively.

> **'Credibility comprises the objective and subjective components of the believability of a source or message.'**

We may further consider credibility in terms of the capability, knowledge, or expertise that a person has.

Activity

Think of a relationship where you currently perceive there is limited, little or, even, no trust.

Consider this relationship based only on the two definitions above and then answer the three questions below:

1 Which of the elements is missing in that relationship?

2 What could you or the other person/s potentially do to change or improve this deficiency?

3 What actions could you take to bring this about?

Being more trusted and more trusting of others does require an entirely different perspective. We need to make some additional effort ourselves, and we need to use much more of our emotional intelligence.

Go back on your answers to the questions above and ask yourself what would have happened if you were behaving ethically, honestly and with a hefty dose of emotional intelligence.

Consider that, rather than taking the moral high ground, where the lack of trust was created by them and not you, there is an alternative perspective and that they were just behaving as themselves.

In other words, they were just doing what they were programmed to do, using the behaviours and limited knowledge or capability that they currently believe is right for that situation.

The emotional intelligence approach is not to assume anything about another person. Instead, it requires us to understand that they may well, just like ourselves, have numerous imperfections.

Wherever possible, we need to acknowledge this fact or at least try to help them remedy those things, without becoming condescending or patronising.

The best way to achieve this is by using an open questioning approach, by asking questions that help eliminate our assumptions of them or the situation.

By 'listening to understand', we enrich our knowledge of the situation, and we will be helping them to unlock any issues or problems and, thereby, effectively coaching them to find better solutions.

Just as in coaching, the secret is to ask them the questions and let them find solutions themselves by not telling them the answers. It is more challenging work for us to begin with, although the benefits far outweigh the effort we have to put in.

The best CEO I ever worked for started each new conversation he had with me, irrespective of whether we were in his office, the boardroom or just sharing a lift, by asking me a new open question.

'What's happening in the XYZ space at the moment, Phil?' He might ask. (The focus is on a specific area of the business I was running.)

Once I had answered, he then gently moved onto deeper questioning by asking, *'Why are we not doing more of X?'* (The focus is on current and proposed actions.)

And, once I managed to explain that, he would then ask, *'So what could you do to increase Y?'* (The focus is on an alternative, a possibility or even a radical new approach.)

Simple, practical, and very smart. My meetings with that CEO were often very concise and always gave me something to work on in terms of my personal development, let alone significantly helping me to improve the profitability of my division.

Conscientiousness

We may consider that conscientiousness is knowing what is right and thereby acting with great care. It may also portray a personality trait like being honest, careful or prudent. Some might like to add that it displays characteristics of being diligent, reliable and hard-working.

In contrast, others may consider those conscientious people as sticklers, perfectionists, workaholics and potentially overly compulsive in their behaviour.

Whichever side of the fence we choose to sit, we all need some of these characteristics and, if we do not believe that we currently have them, it is going to be pretty handy in knowing where to find them.

The more radical and spontaneous we are inclined, the more we will need to generate that balancing perspective of a conscientious and, possibly, more considered approach.

Yet, we do not want for that more careful approach to be so constrictive that our creativity becomes hampered by it!

This aspect is one of the most significant issues faced by many of my clients. The battle between the analytical and the creative, the cautious and the extravagant, the considered and the unconsidered.

The yin and yang of these traits are evident in business, politics, social groups and families, and they are even going on daily inside our heads. Our unique preferences are those things that separate the left side, and the right side, the analytical and the creative parts of our brain.

Each of the choices we make, moment by moment, calls into action, more or less of an analytical or creative bunch of neurons. While some of us may prefer an innovative solution, we also have equal access to a systematic approach and vice versa.

Although, for many of us, we choose not to consider the other potentially balancing perspective, because we have convinced or programmed ourselves that we are more analytical or creative, often denying ourselves a fully balanced view.

Conscientiousness is about creating the right internal balance between these two often conflicting thought processes and not allowing one to outdo the other.

For many of us, our creative or analytical internal programming constrains us, it limits our ability to balance the alternative perspective and, thereby, potentially inhibits the outcome of our actions. A more conscientious approach is to have always considered both sides in our brain before deciding on a new course of action!

One way to rectify this might be to consider the situation from a completely different standpoint. It may help us to step into the metaphorical shoes of a person who is opposite to us.

In other words, if we are creative, we need to choose someone more analytically minded and, if our preference is to be analytical, we select someone more creative.

Now, consider their perspective. What would they see, hear and feel about this situation? What type of actions might they take? What might the total opposite of our current approach be?

How we view the situation after considering a more conscientious approach will have a significant impact on the result we attain. Even if we do not find an alternative approach ourselves, we will, undoubtedly, have taken a more conscientious thought process.

Activity

Are you more creative or analytical in your approach? How might it feel if you were to consider an issue using both perspectives, the whole of your brain, rather than more of one side than the other?

Using a conscientious approach, consider a current challenge or situation and then imagine that you are asking three people whom you admire to help you solve the problem.

- Ideally, think of people who may not have the same creative or analytical perspective as yourself, and try to think of people who are opposite, different, or will even be challenging in their views.

- What would you imagine they recommend, what actions might they suggest? Or imagine how they might go about getting the best result if they were in your shoes.

chapter 5

———

Self-management

What is it?

The self-management dimension traditionally describes how we each take responsibility for our behaviours and wellbeing. However, in terms of emotional intelligence, it goes beyond this to encompass how we manage the day-to-day relationship we have with ourselves as well as with other people. The self-management dimension covers:

- Drive
- Commitment
- Optimism

Your dimension feedback

Use the *average* score that you recorded for this particular PEIP dimension to review the relevant feedback, as detailed by the corresponding levels of 1 to 6 below.

Level 1: Unmotivated – Undedicated – Cynical

You demonstrate an isolated approach to self-management whereby you only commit to doing something to better yourself when you have a pressing reason or in the case of a deadline. You sometimes just simply cannot be bothered to do things, especially when you are having one of your more cynical days, possibly resulting in a general lack of motivation and thereby a potential lack of accomplishment.

Level 2: Trivialise – Guarded – Negative

You appear to be quite guarded and self-focused, your negativity identifies that you are not entirely bothered by the requirements or needs of other people, who will, in return, likely have negative feelings about you. Also, while you may make plans, these will rarely include specific actions or accountabilities for yourself or others.

Level 3: Enthusiastic – Dedicated – Opportunistic

You show a high level of commitment towards other people through demonstrating a dedicated, albeit slightly opportunistic, attitude. You might need to be mindful of seeing the bigger picture for others as well as for yourself and being prepared to flex your behaviours more to suit the situation or goal.

Level 4: Focused – Balanced – Positive

You demonstrate a reasonable level of focus towards the task and people management aspects of your life. You balance your commitment towards both elements well. However, you may need to provide yourself with a more positive mental framework to work in, similar, possibly, to the one you already offer to others.

Level 5: Achievable – Commitment – Pragmatic

You are reliable and dependable because you fully comprehend what is realistic and achievable in most situations. You are committed to your own and others' success, and you pragmatically and diligently work towards achieving joint outcomes.

Level 6: Driven – Committed – Inspiring

You are very likely to be highly entrepreneurial by nature; once a new possibility inspires your imagination, you are committed and will stop at nothing to make sure that it happens. Your energy and enthusiasm will inspire other people to follow you willingly.

Developing your EI in this dimension

Drive

To determine what drives us, we may need to consider those innate, biological stimuli or urges that we generate to attain a goal or merely to satisfy a specific need. Sometimes, the goal stimulus can be so enormous that people become consumed by it.

Think of Nobel Prize Winners like Mother Teresa. In 1950, she founded the Missionaries of Charity in pursuit of a goal to provide the necessities for the lives of those impoverished. The charity grew to become active in 133 countries, employing more than 4,500 nuns.

Or, former President of South Africa, anti-apartheid revolutionary, philanthropist and 27-year prisoner, Nelson Mandela, who pursued the vision of freedom for black South Africans.

Think also of Mahatma Gandhi, who may not have received a Nobel Prize, although he did become the *Father Of An Independent Nation* through his absolute pursuit of truth and non-violence-based ideals.

All these people, and many more of our most exceptional human beings, have one thing in common, and that is a vision or goal to achieve something far beyond themselves.

Throughout history, there have also been many despots, tyrants and oppressors whom, it would seem, have only ever been motivated by a self-serving vision of their reality of a specific need.

Let us be quite clear here; there is a difference between satisfying an apparent need and fulfilling a worthy goal or a more significant vision. The difference is that needs tend to be more personally focused, whereas goals should be universal.

I am not trying to imply that our goals should be so big that they will have a profound effect on humanity, although there is nothing wrong with that. What I am advocating is that if we only focus goals on our personal needs, then we may negate realising all the benefits of having the appropriate drive to achieve them effectively.

Let us imagine that we focus solely on our need for increasing our level of income and the possibility of earning more money is what drives us. We put in extra effort, we work ridiculous hours, we spend more time at work than at home, we may even have taken a second job. And, eventually, we may start to get better financial results for our efforts.

Our boss recognises the contribution we have made and gives us a bonus or a pay rise. We have made more money, so the need has been satisfied.

Or has it?

The decision is then to continue bringing increasing amounts of stress on ourselves and our family to keep up that new level of income, or to revert to how we used to do things previously with a lot less stress.

We all know what happens. We take the more challenging option or, instead, it is often made by someone else who has benefited from our increased endeavours and thereby encourages us to do more and more.

Increased stress results in high blood pressure, which may lead to a potential risk of a heart attack or stroke. Increased stress also contributes to the many anxiety-related mental health conditions we hear reported every day.

When our focus is on a much broader goal, like improving the quality of life for our family, then the drive to achieve this would itself become different. This more general goal will need to include more than just money needs. It might involve drivers or conditions, like spending more quality time with our children or our parents.

It might consist of training up a member of our team to handle some of our extra workloads so that we can get home earlier a few days a week. It might even mean that we must learn new skills to become a more effective manager or team member and thus enable each person in our team to accomplish considerably more than they could achieve alone.

The result is that our income and quality of life will improve and, although it might take a little longer to achieve, it will also significantly enhance the lives of all the people involved.

Remember that the broader the target, the more opportunity there is of us hitting it. For a goal to be truly useful, it must satisfy more than just a single need.

Consequently, if we wish to bring an entire vision into reality, we must ensure that it has both interrelated and meaningful goals within it.

Activity

1 Start by thinking about a meaningful goal and not just an apparent or current need. (Having a better quality of life, as opposed to only earning more money.)

2 Identify the individual drivers that will make up this goal.

3 Consider which of these drivers is self-focused and which are universal.

4 Remove any self-focused drivers.

5 Focus your attention on each of the universal drivers and consider how these may play out, what you may have to start or stop doing differently and how you might bring this about.

6 Ask yourself if this goal is realistic, achievable and has a completion date. If you answer no to any of this, start again.

7 Create a plan, identify actionable results, and set deadlines.

8 Set to work on achieving this goal.

Commitment

Being dedicated to a cause or even a goal does not mean that we should always have a virtuous reason for the direction we choose to take.

In terms of commitment, I do rather like the analogy of showing strong loyalty and positive support, resulting in affirmative action towards someone or something other than ourselves.

Commitment is not just something we keep in our heads; it needs to be displayed and felt by other people as well. The more committed we are towards our goals or ideals, and the more we share that commitment with others, the more they will be on board with our thinking and the likelihood of achievement increases.

The trouble is that if we become overly obsessed with our commitment towards a subject, we may end up preaching our ideals and not effectively living them.

I have seen this happen so many times, where the manager of a team attends one of my workshops, they learn something new, and they are 100 per cent committed to putting it into action when they go back to work.

A few weeks later, I hear that the first thing the manager did when they got back to work was to bring their team together, tell them of all the fantastic advantages and benefits of the new knowledge and then expect them to put it into practice!

I often quote that *'The first rule of leadership is to go there first.'* In other words, do not expect someone else to adopt a new way of thinking or being, without being committed to doing it ourselves!

Commitment is far more significant than just a state of mind; it requires action, follow-up and feedback. When we demonstrate commitment, it is something we show others through adopting a set of behaviours that reflect that commitment.

Think of the last time someone let us down. What clues did they give us that they were not as committed towards the goal as we were? There are many subtle signs, both emotional and physical, that will tell us that someone is not entirely committed to our idea or goal.

Some clues that we can pick up on during a conversation may include (although will not be limited to) some or all the following:

- Negative language patterns – we will hear words such as cannot, shan't, won't, don't and no, but included within their dialogue.

- The eyes have it – their heads may be nodding yes, while their eyes are saying no, as they will not be comfortable making direct eye contact with us.

- Eyes narrowing – a slight narrowing of the eyes is an instinctual, universal expression of aggression, anger or non-conformity.

Note: some people may choose to do this as a way of trying to show that they are thinking, which often can result in misunderstanding.

- Chin stroking – people often will stroke their chins during the decision-making process, potentially sending the message of I am judging you, or I do not believe you.

- Body block – notebooks, handbags, papers, cups, mobile phones, and indeed anything else, held in front of their body or face indicates either shyness or resistance.

- Face touching – especially the nose, can indicate deception, or covering up the mouth when talking is a gesture usually associated with lying.

- Checking themselves – fingernails, the time, or picking off bits of fluff from clothing often indicates disapproval of an idea or concept.

- Fake smile – a genuine smile wrinkles the corners of the eyes and, as a result, changes the expression of the entire face.

- Leaning away – often, when a person becomes bored or disinterested, they will lean away from the speaker.

- Crossing arms – this is an instinctive defensive resistance posture that may also portray egotism. Be mindful, though, that they may have physical problems. Sometimes, people cross their arms when they are relaxed and interested because it is more comfortable.

- Scratching the head – this is a very typical display of doubt or uncertainty.

- Increased blinking – increased heart rate and breathing faster are all early signs of anxiety.

- Shifting body weight from foot to foot – often indicates mental or physical discomfort.

- Playing with the collar of a shirt or blouse – usually associated with feeling uncomfortable or nervous.

Note: these are only some general examples of types of body language and do not necessarily always reflect different cultural or environmental circumstances.

When commitment is not present in us, we subconsciously demonstrate it to others through the subtle nature of the posture, words and actions we use. The more emotionally intelligent the other person is, the more likelihood there is of them picking up on our lack of commitment.

When we start to observe ourselves and others in different contextual situations accurately, we begin to gain a pronounced ability to change the way we behave and, thereby, respond, as a result.

Activity

Take some time to consider how your commitment shows up when you are engaged in discussion with another person.

Note: the conversation does not have to be face-to-face; it may well be over the phone, or virtually via the web.

- What particular words or phrases are you most likely to use when you are committed to something and for when you are not?

- What is your fully committed posture? Where are your hands, what are they doing? Where are your shoulders, eyes, head and feet?

- What is your position when you do not have any commitment?

- What do you hear when you show your commitment to something, and what do you hear when you do not? Please try to be objective with this one as it is easy to think only from a prejudiced viewpoint.

- How do you feel when you are not committed to something? Try to think of all your emotional states, those displayed physically as well as those experienced internally.

- What specifically do you need to change?

Optimism

Winston Churchill once said that a pessimist sees the difficulty in every opportunity, while an optimist sees opportunity in every difficulty. I think that helps us to define what we are talking about in this element.

We have all encountered the naysayers of this world, the seemingly unfriendly people who appear to live in a perpetual pessimistic state. They oppose, object or criticise every single aspect of an idea or change, irrespective of whether it relates directly to themselves or not.

In contrast, we also know those people who are eternal optimists, who always see good in everything and everyone, irrespective of the situation.

To understand why they are like this, we need to understand what is going on inside their heads. According to Professor Tim Spector, of St Thomas' Hospital in London, who has done extensive research into why people are more optimistic about life than others, it is partly down to *epigenetics*.

His studies suggest that when it comes to personality, half of the differences between us are genetic, and five of the genes located in the hippocampus (middle part of our brain) become modified, dialled up or dialled down (called *epigenetics*) throughout our lives in response to environmental factors.

Spector goes on to say that the adage of 'we can't change' has now been updated by the knowledge that we can, indeed, modify and even take control of our so-called genetic behaviour.

Further studies suggest that there is a significant correlation between health, wellness and optimism. Following several years of research, Professor Becca Levy of Yale University concluded that those people who had felt the most optimistic about growing older had lived, on average, around seven and a half years longer than those who were more pessimistic.

We do not need to be research scientists to fully recognise and understand the essential links to our health of depression, anxiety and stress with pessimism.

Before we become too embroiled into the adverse effects of a pessimistic attitude, let me point out that there is a big difference in being cautious towards something as opposed to being sceptical or cynical about it.

Being cautious tends to be based on good judgement or careful deliberation, where a sceptic is more likely to question or have suspicion of others' opinions and a cynic will believe that people act only in self-interest.

There are some outstanding benefits in having a positive and optimistic mindset:

- Better health – optimism boosts our immune system. Pessimistic people have twice as many health-related infectious illnesses and visit their doctors twice as much for other health-related issues.

- Improved relationships – better mood control, higher self-regard and positivity all encourage the sharing of positive emotions, which generate better relationships.

- Happier self – positive people imagine positive outcomes and comfortably work towards these. When we are positive, the central nervous system and the pituitary gland release endorphins into the brain, which act on the opiate receptors, which reduce pain and boost pleasure.

- Better coping mechanisms – when we are in a positive mindset, we make decisions faster, we reduce internal negative dialogue, we accept challenges and find solutions.

- Higher performance – optimists appear to exert more effort towards achieving their objectives and reduce negative stress by removing physical or emotional inertia.

Becoming more optimistic is not as simple as turning on a different switch in our brain, even if we knew where to find one. It requires a complete review and re-evaluation as to how we choose to live our life.

We might start with the end in mind, by considering what a more positive and confident person with our unique skills and ability might achieve.

Then, we might consider those aspects that we might currently be holding back and then start to work on each of the conversations we have, paying strict attention to those that begin inside our head.

The six levels of emotional efficacy, which I have used to form the basis of the PEIP assessment and this book, each relate to the levels of internal belief that we employ concerning our ability to navigate and live our emotional lives successfully.

For example, high emotional efficacy enables us to deal efficiently with challenging emotions; we regulate these by choosing healthy coping mechanisms from which we can express our values through our choice of positive actions.

Alternatively, when we have low levels of emotional efficacy, we might become entrenched in patterns of negative, detrimental and otherwise maladaptive behavioural responses.

Activity

Using my *six levels of emotional efficacy* (found at the beginning of Part 2) might help you to work through any conflicting negative thoughts, words and actions that may be holding you back from developing a more optimistic outlook.

chapter 6

Influencing others

What is it?

The influence dimension relates directly to our ability in affecting the behaviours, developments and characteristics of a person, thing, or situation. Influence can, therefore, be as small as an intimate gesture between two people or as global as an astronomical event.

The influence dimension covers:

- Motivation
- Leveraging diversity
- Political awareness

Your dimension feedback

Use the *average* score that you recorded for this particular PEIP dimension to review the relevant feedback, as detailed by the corresponding levels of 1 to 6 below.

Level 1: Unmotivated – Unaware – Disconnected

You demonstrate a lack of personal motivation. You also show unawareness of other people and their differences, as well as being disconnected from the realities of business and social contexts; you might not be surprised to find that any influence you have is likely to be rated as ineffective.

Level 2: Impressionable – Complacent – Condescending

You may well appear to be impressionable to some people. Enjoying an uncritical satisfaction with yourself or from your achievements may also lead to you becoming condescending towards other ideals, demonstrating that you are likely to have only a very passive level of influence.

Level 3: Status – Respect – Practical

Because status is essential to you, the respect you show for others may, to some extent, become compromised and your practical realisation of how things work within your world might also become influenced by it. As a result, your overall level of influence is most likely to be quite low-key.

Level 4: Support – Collaborate – Savvy

The support you afford other people is commendable, and the level of collaboration that this encourages is vital in ensuring that people are fairly treated and well managed. Your broad understanding of the political landscape demonstrates a competent level of influence.

Level 5: Excited – Manage – Persuade

Your ability to engage and excite people towards any goal while effectively managing their collective or individual differences is outstanding, which is why your level of influence is very persuasive.

Level 6: Motivated – Inclusive – Awareness

The high level of personal motivation and the total flexibility you model around the awareness and integration of all human ability within each aspect of your world is exemplary, resulting in a seldom bettered level of 'authority' concerning your influencing skills.

Developing your EI in this dimension

Motivation

Motivation is the union of internal impulses; those thoughts that enable a person to action, move towards or away from a goal.

When we meet with an influencer who is highly motivated, it is easy to be swept along by their enthusiasm. An influencer's commitment to achieve a goal can be so infectious that we may abandon our own more mediocre plans to jump on board with theirs.

Our motivation is not always steady, constant, or even consistent. Our mood, our level of enjoyment or lack of it will influence it, together with the pressures of our everyday lives.

How we gain the right motivation and then manage to maintain it, day in and day out, even in the face of adversity, is one of the most challenging aspects that govern our future success or failure.

Motivation happens inside our brain when our levels of dopamine increase. Dopamine is a neurotransmitter, sometimes referred to as a chemical messenger, produced in our bodies, and plays a role in how we feel pleasure, think, plan, strive and focus.

We are addicted to this wonder chemical; it makes us feel good, so the more we can replicate a positive experience, the better we can engage with it.

In a study by Vanderbilt University, a form of brain mapping was used to identify the levels of dopamine present in certain parts of the brains of 'go-getters' and 'slackers'.

The results showed that the 'go-getters' had higher levels of dopamine in the reward and motivation part of their brain.

In comparison, the 'slackers', interestingly, showed higher levels of dopamine in the part of the brain associated with emotion and risk.

The conclusion was that, to understand the science of motivation, one needed to regard dopamine levels in different parts of the brain and how they influenced behaviour in times of pleasure as well as in times of stress, pain and loss. A dopamine deficiency results in people being less likely to work towards something.

Studies further show that low levels in dopamine are also responsible for lack of interest, procrastination, poor sleep patterns, fatigue, excessive feelings of hopelessness, with decreased motivation, potentially leading to depression.

There are a few simple techniques we can introduce into our lives to increase our level of dopamine and ensure it works in the right parts of our brain at the correct times:

- Staying positive and upbeat increases dopamine levels. The more positive and optimistic we remain, even in trying circumstances, the more dopamine is released.

- Setting realistic and incrementally achievable goals allows for a continual release of dopamine, into the reward and motivation pre-frontal cortex part of our brain.

- Having clear, positive, internal dialogue reduces the dopamine receptors in the anterior cingulate cortex, resulting in less negative emotional feeling associated with risk and uncertainty, and produces higher dopamine levels in the pre-frontal cortex.

- Creating a solid plan and sticking to it, celebrating success, and positively acknowledging any failure, substantially increases dopamine levels.

- Reducing sugar intake; sugar alters our brain chemistry directly by interrupting the production of dopamine, reducing the transient 'high' that we feel from sugar will increase the longer-term 'high' we get from dopamine.

- Staying focused towards goals also increases dopamine levels. Check in regularly with ourselves to ensure we are on track and positively reward ourselves for each successful step we take.

- Being happy releases a draught of positive endorphins and neurotransmitters, which increase the dopamine and opiate receptors across our brain, making us feel alive and amazing!

Motivating others

Motivating others must start with driving yourself first. If you are not motivated, you cannot expect others to be. Remember: *'The first rule of leadership is to go there first.'*

I cannot begin to count the number of times I have heard managers instruct their teams to do more to reach an impossible goal when, so clearly, they are not motivated towards it themselves.

Be realistic. If the original goal is just too big to achieve, chunk it down into bite-sized, manageable steps and then engage with the whole team on how the collective *'we'* can make each step work.

Celebrate success with every member of the team and not just the ones who completed a step towards the goal. On achieving each new milestone, the higher levels of dopamine experienced across the group will enhance the experience for everyone, making the next challenge easier.

The long-term results will be a lot more favourable as each team member will have taken some new level of ownership and responsibility in working towards the final goal.

Activity

Take some time out to reflect on where your motivation currently is, how it manifests and what elements you might need
to focus on to make it work better for you and, thereby, potentially for others.

Identify a realistic, trackable, short-term, specific goal,
and plan how you will achieve this. Be courageous without being unrealistic, set yourself an achievable time scale
and put markers in place to measure your progress at each
stage.

Prepare to celebrate. Ensure that you have included a
reward for when you reach every milestone, as this will
increase your dopamine levels and, thereby, help you to
achieve the larger goal faster.

Leveraging diversity

One would like to imagine that, in today's multi-cultural, multi-
media world, we all have a good appreciation of the extensive and
incredible diversification that exists across all human society. We
would also like to believe that gone are the days of age, sex, race,
cultural or religious bias being a problem.

Unfortunately, this is not the case. We still hear of racial abuse
and segregation within communities or disharmony within
sub-cultures due to gender, religious, social, ethnic, sexual orientation, socio-economic status, age, physical ability, political and,
indeed, many other preferences that I may well have missed.

We only have to turn on our TVs to hear and see the latest racial
or ethnical preference stories. Yet, so much more than colour or race
is going on behind those reported scenes. For example, when any
disenfranchised 'minority' group gets selected airtime, this means
that the people who belong within a 'majority' group are likewise
being segregated-out because of those preferences.

And, what about all those unchallenged behaviours in the way
that many large corporates still recruit staff, where, during their

standard application process, individuals have to respond to questions like 'Did your parents attend university?'? This, as I am sure you will agree, only sends the message to the applicant that if your parents did not go to university, then we are not going to be interested in pursuing your application!

Furthermore, what about all of those unreported stories where people are still not being recruited because of their age, as the organisation doing the recruiting prefers to look for 'bright young things' with little or no proven experience, as opposed to mature adults with decades of expertise and tonnes of proven capability?

Our preferences shape who we are as well as who we are comfortable in being with, and it is those preferences that we need to challenge as human beings the world over if we are ever going to accept that we are *all* different!

Before we begin to condemn or condone anyone for being a miscreant towards any form of inclusion, we must first endeavour to understand why any such inclusion preference was not there in the first place.

Let us go back to our prehistoric brains and consider what is going on below the cerebral cortex and why one person is more likely to be less inclusive than another.

When we meet a person for the first time, we start to make assumptions about them, often without being consciously aware that we are even doing this.

Our brain uses these first impressions to create a preference for people who are most like us. These preferences go on to shape our beliefs and behaviours towards that other person.

The brain is hard-wired to connect easily with people who appear similar, and these similar characteristics might include race, colour, religion, gender, or any other non-deviation from our current preference of the world.

Whether we like it or not, we are under the influence of *implicit bias* – a conscious or subconscious bias that we may automatically activate when meeting people who are different from our implicit preferences.

The reason why this happens is mainly due to the original concepts of 'tribe' mentality, implying the possession of a strong, familiar, family, cultural or ethnic identity that separates one member of a group from the members of another. There will, entirely naturally, be those implications relating to the protection of the tribe from any real or perceived threats.

The problem we have today is removing the association of a new or a different person with that of a potential threat. The assumptions we make about other people are part of that defence mechanism which, as we have already discussed, are no longer relevant in modern society.

We can help to minimise those assumptions by switching our thoughts to an enquiry mode. In other words, we ask open questions that elicit a state of 'wanting to understand' rather than assuming we 'already know' and thereby changing our preferences.

This approach increases engagement for both parties; it removes any preconceived ideas and thereby encourages an inclusive framework for a cooperative and mutually beneficial way forward.

The many problems we hear about relating to diversity and inclusion are due to one party not bothering to understand the other party's unique perspectives, or preferences entirely. Assumptions are made, sometimes on both sides and, before too long, the prehistoric brain kicks in and, subsequently, the tribal mentality then creates disharmony.

Today, we need diversity more than ever; rationalising our changing world of work through using a multi-faceted approach, requires using an ever more diverse set of skills, ages, knowledge, experience and abilities.

Many of those capabilities likely will not be within our existing 'tribal' consciousness; we will need to seek them outside of our traditional comfort areas and encourage participation from all communities.

Activity

Review a situation where you may have been more inclined to stick to a 'tribal' rationale or a set of preferences that may have excluded rather than included a wider demographic of people, and consider what alternative approaches you may have uncovered if you had asked more open questions from a wider perspective.

It may help you to read the techniques I cover for open questioning in Chapter 8 Developing others plus, to get you started, ask yourself all the following questions:

- How do your current preferences affect the relationships you have with the people you know well?
- How do those current preferences affect how you develop new relationships with other people?
- How do your current preferences affect the relationship you have with yourself?
- What preferences do you specifically need to work on, and when are you going to do something about it?

I would encourage you to go a step further, no matter how uncomfortable this might be, and consider how your unconscious bias and preferences shape every aspect of the way you live and work. Ultimately, so that you may no longer become part of any injustice that might perpetuate the problem.

Political awareness

Politics will, inevitably, happen in all groups or collections of people, irrespective of the group's size or purpose.

Being politically aware is about gaining a deeper knowledge of the more subtle influences that shape group culture and then, maybe, using that knowledge, it will help us to steer the group towards a mutually favourable outcome.

When politics are working well, they create the unseen unity of flow that exists just beneath the surface within a group, and help it maintain a forward trajectory towards its ultimate purpose.

When politics are not working well, they create upheaval and turbulence, caused by hidden agendas, indecision, uncertainty and frustration, which ultimately lead to total disengagement of some or all members of the group.

It is, therefore, easy to consider political awareness initially as a force for personal gain, where unscrupulous individuals play at organisational politics to manipulate others towards their chosen objectives.

Political awareness, though, can also be a force for good and, if used wisely, it can help an entire organisation of people reach their full potential.

The adage of *'how things get done around here'* might, for example, serve to help us understand the reasons why there may be blockages within the system itself, as opposed to finding a short cut that may be temporarily useful in meeting our private agenda.

Political awareness is not just a matter of personal choice; it is becoming an ever more critical tool in helping us discern why things are working well and what we may need to focus our attention on when they are not.

Becoming more politically aware is about tuning in and hearing the real messages behind the words that people use and seeing the behaviours that people adopt. It encourages us to go further in reading the subtle signs that people are unhappy with a new course of action and knowing when to take the appropriate steps to help, encourage and support them.

The essential aspect of being politically aware is not to have any hidden agenda; if we must have an agenda at all, it needs to have a universal benefit and be shared openly with everyone.

Imagine a situation where an individual within the team we managed had a hidden agenda. They wanted our job, irrespective of whether they could do it or not.

Suppose that we were not able to identify the signs that this person was working surreptitiously behind the scenes to discredit us. Then, over a period of months, we might be entirely shocked when an affable member of our team finally lets us know what is going on.

We may then find ourself with a similar problem of trying to catch a herd of horses after they have bolted through the gate that we had unintentionally left open.

Analogies aside, if only we were able to read the very subtle shifts in the team's dynamic, like the small changes in behaviour or some trusted people no longer making direct eye contact with us. Or, we may have picked up on the discrete language or word changes in conversations when we entered or left the room.

We would also have been able to identify the potential issue early enough and then quickly have been able to deal with it at its source.

No doubt, as a politically aware leader, we would have encouraged the individual through open conversation to describe where they saw their future within the team. Over time, and, if realistic, you would then work with them to develop a plan to help them achieve that goal or, at the very least, a goal aligned against their potential.

Political awareness is about being emotionally intelligent, all the time. Being able to read, identify and translate the subtle ebb and flow of human behaviour will, undoubtedly, support us across all aspects of our life.

Activity

- How politically aware are you currently and what are the current implications of that awareness on the people around you?

- What might you start doing differently to become more in tune with the broader organisational, social and political context?

- What political currents exist in your work or private life that may be indicative of problems just sitting beneath the surface?

- How might you start to resolve these?

chapter 7

——

Improving stakeholder relationships

What is it?

A stakeholder is anyone who is directly affected by what you do; these will be people at home as well as those at work. The stakeholder management dimension regards the continuous process of maintaining relationships with the people who have an impact across all the various aspects of our lives.

Communicating effectively with each of these stakeholders, in a way that is appropriate, meaningful to them and not necessarily for ourselves, is essential to ensuring that they remain fully engaged and supportive of our endeavours.

The stakeholder management dimension covers:

- Stakeholder perception
- Stakeholder orientation
- Stakeholder engagement

Your dimension feedback

Use the *average* score that you recorded for this particular PEIP dimension to review the relevant feedback, as detailed by the corresponding levels of 1 to 6 below.

Level 1: Unclear – Limited – Unengaging

There is a lack of clarity in understanding who your stakeholders might be. You potentially have a low perception of their specific needs and wants, combined with minimal engagement. It is highly likely that there will be a level of apprehension experienced by all parties involved on both sides of your communications.

Level 2: Assumptive – Knowledge – Challenging

You have based your stakeholder engagement upon a series of assumptions; these assumptions will, inevitably, lead to a poor knowledge of your stakeholders' specific needs, which is likely to result in many of your essential relationships becoming challenging and potentially regarded as superficial.

Level 3: Separate – Inflexible – Broad

While you may perceive that your level of stakeholder management is reasonable to good, there is a possibility that your actual knowledge of your stakeholders' requirements is limited. Through adopting an inflexible approach in determining individual, specific, current, or future needs, you will not be adapting enough to their situation.

Level 4: Comprehensive – Adaptable – Understanding

You demonstrate a comprehensive acumen with regards to your stakeholders; you adapt to some of their changing requirements and provide a reasonable level of understanding concerning their situation.

Level 5: Assess – Respond – Accommodate

You remain conscious of your stakeholders' needs in many situations; you spend time assessing each aspect of their unique requirements and consistently strive to accommodate them by responding effectively to each new situation.

Level 6: Perceptive – Intuitive – Improvement

You continuously seek to excite your stakeholders because you are highly perceptive to their actual requirements; you use a healthy level of intuition to help guide and shape how the relationship might continuously be improved and developed.

Developing your EI in this dimension

Stakeholder perception

You are one of my stakeholders. You have purchased my book, and that makes you a part of what I do, whether you are a customer, client, friend, colleague, associate, a member of my family, or my publisher, you are a stakeholder.

Stakeholders are an essential part of my writing and business success. Therefore, you have become very important to me!

The perception I have developed about you is crucial in determining how I write the words I write. If I were not to write in a way that measured up to my perception of you, then I will be doing us both a disservice.

You could become so disenchanted with the book that you throw it away and only ever mention it to others, warning them not also to waste their hard-earned money. And, thus, turning you from stakeholder to antagonist.

However, my perception of you is that you are naturally curious; you want to improve your lot in life and maybe even become a better person because of it.

You are likely to be a person who is intrigued by the power of the human mind and interested in the possibilities of aligning yourself effectively with other people to make a lasting and positive difference to your world.

You may equally be reading this because of some feedback that suggested that you needed to become more emotionally aware.

How do I know all of this? The answer is that we spent a great deal of time in crafting the material for this book in appealing to those people who fitted the above perception.

If my perception of you is wrong, then we have both made a mistake, you have purchased the wrong book, and I have written it for someone else entirely!

The perceptions we make about our stakeholders, not just the ones who are our customers, should influence all our decisions and our behaviours. The problem then only exists if our perceptions become those assumptions founded on a lack of knowledge or any relevant, supporting information.

Perceptions are our way of regarding, interpreting and then understanding something, usually using our five senses, plus, if we are lucky enough to have developed it, our sixth sense, being '*intuition*'. Assumptions are typically related to a fact or statement, considered true or accurate without any proof.

Consider changing 'stakeholder perception' into 'stakeholder assumption', and we may understand why so many costly marketing and business mistakes happen.

It may also give us some idea about why some of those engagements with other stakeholders, like our boss, members of our team, friends, family, in fact, anyone who has a stake in what we do, sometimes do not go to plan.

Merely turning our assumptions into perceptions will give us the heads-up on what may be going on in a situation. It will ensure that we can make amendments that will result in a more positive outcome for all concerned parties.

An example of this might be a situation where your boss has asked you to compile a report, let us say, on how to reduce staff turnover. You are excited by the prospect of dealing with a meaty and worthwhile topic, especially as the department is under increasing pressure to do more, with ever decreasing numbers of staff.

After speaking with some of the remaining more senior members of the team, you surmise that the principal reason why people are leaving is down to low salary levels, or that they are just not the right personality 'type' for the department.

Based on the *assumptions* you have made, you conclude that salary levels across the team should rise and that the whole team needs to be involved in the recruitment process.

You write everything up and then prepare to present your report to your manager and expect to be congratulated on a job well done. Except, that is not what happens. Your manager asks you before you even sit down to present your report, a very straightforward question, and that is 'How many of the leavers did you manage to speak with?'

If you had only spoken with a few of the leavers, you might have had a very different report. Because the *perception* of the leavers was that, although the salary levels were comparatively low, the benefits package the company provides is excellent and more than makes up for the lower salary.

The other *perception* that the leavers had was that some longer-serving members of the team were lazy and often foisted additional work onto new or more junior members of staff so that they could get out of work early and spend more time socialising!

Going beyond the pursuit of excellence in serving our stakeholders is one of the critical ingredients for a successful business. If we focus only on assumptions, we will continue to make costly mistakes.

That means that we must engage *with* our stakeholders verbally and, if that's not possible, at the very least, ensure that we are basing our perceptions on some reality of proof.

Activity

1 What assumptions have you already made about one of your most important stakeholders? (N.B. an assumption is a proposition taken for granted, without any basis of real evidence or fact.)

2 What is your perception of their actual wants and needs?

3 How much variance is there between your assumptions and your perceptions?

4 What do you need to start doing differently?

Stakeholder orientation

Stakeholder orientation describes a model of social responsibility, where the way we act, behave and the decisions we make are in the best interests of all our stakeholders.

While many people will agree that this is often easier said than done, we cannot disagree with the sentiment of wanting to do right by everyone.

The problem is that we let our 'selves' get in the way. In other words, we tend to focus on our wants and needs before we begin to consider those of other people.

My second rule of leadership is '*Make it about them and not about yourself.*' Which, by the way, also serves in sales, marketing, customer relations, HR, finance, and across all other human activities, even in parenting!

We know those self-serving people, who do not care about anyone or anything, whose perspective in life is to fill their boots with as much as they can possibly cram in.

We also may know those self-sacrificing people who would genuinely give away everything they have just to help another person. Which, although praiseworthy, may possibly lead to them being homeless and destitute.

Of course, there needs to be a balance between self-serving and self-sacrificing, and that is what I want to focus on here in stakeholder orientation.

A way to view this topic is that everyone who has a stake in what you do is a stakeholder, and that includes yourself. Aligning the needs and wants of others with our own needs and wants is often where most issues arise. Let's consider a typical example of where this may cause some friction.

Your boss has asked you to stay late to help her compile a report required for a board meeting, taking place, first thing tomorrow morning.

Your boss seldom makes these types of requests of you and appears to be under a fair amount of pressure and is certainly not behaving in her usual happy way, so this board meeting is significant.

The problem you have is that you have already arranged to meet with an old friend, who is visiting for only one day before flying back home to South Africa, where their family emigrated three years ago.

The conundrum is that you want to do both: help your boss, and meet your friend. To compound the issue further, you have no way of contacting your friend, and your boss is waiting for an answer.

What would you do?

These types of situations pop up in all areas of our lives, and often we must make an instant decision, which may mean that one or other of the parties concerned is likely to be losing out.

Or does it?

Consider the same situation using four valuable tools that you have at your disposal, 'perception', 'honesty', 'creativity' and 'compromise'. How might you reach an amicable position where you can help your boss and meet with your friend on time?

1 What is your 'stakeholder *perception*' based on the facts, having already removed any of your assumptions?

2 Be '*honest*' with the stakeholder/s you can engage with and explain your conundrum.

3 Ask them to help you to find a '*creative*' solution that would help them and you.

4 Always be prepared to '*compromise*'.

Activity

Think of a similar situation you may have had where you ended up having to let at least one of your stakeholders down.

- How did that make you feel, specifically?
- What could you have done to improve this situation?
- What do you need to focus on moving forward?

Stakeholder engagement

Balancing the needs and wants of every one of our stakeholders, including ourselves, is only part of the battle.

The hardest thing to self-manage is to ensure that we present ourselves with each stakeholder in the same way, consistently, day in and day out.

Having first cleared our assumptions out and then replaced them with our perceptions of the reality for each situation, it is then a case of removing the 'persona' we may have inadvertently created about ourselves, thereby leaving a clear open field for the relationships to evolve.

The 'persona' problem is a tough one to deal with, especially if we live a multi-persona type of life. What I mean by this is that we all inhabit the different parts of our lives differently.

How we behave towards our children is likely to be different from how we behave with our partner, or how we conduct ourselves in work or, when socialising, it is likely to be different again.

The simple rule to ensure consistency across our entire lives is to *adapt* according to the situation yet remain *unchanged* at our core. If the nature of our being changes with each interaction, others will, most likely, perceive us as being insincere, flaky, or just downright untrustworthy.

It is, therefore, imperative that we get our core in great shape and that that core is an honest reflection of who we are and whom we want to be, all of the time.

Our core, sometimes referred to as the *essence* of who we are, is derived from our unique values, principles and beliefs. It should be the moral compass from which we steer the inevitably unpredictable course of our lives.

Once we have set our direction or course, it is then a matter of flexing and adapting our behaviours in response to the changing dynamics of a given situation.

Sticking too rigidly to our moral compass and not adapting our behaviours to correct a course will, inevitably, lead us in the wrong direction.

Using a sailing analogy, let us imagine that we are setting sail in a small yacht to Le Havre in France, across the English Channel, from Portsmouth on the south coast of England.

We have set our course by marking a line between Portsmouth and Le Havre on a suitable Admiralty chart. We have then taken a compass bearing of 149.06° as our heading or the direction of travel in which we need to sail. Given the boat's average speed through the water, we estimate getting to Le Havre, in daylight, by early evening. We set sail, and away we go.

After several hours of sailing, keeping to the same compass bearing of 149.06° and, even though we have made good our average speed through the water, we still have no sight of land, and it is starting to get dark.

It is now midnight; we are cold and exhausted, it is pitch black, and there is still no sight of land. Even though we are still following the same compass bearing, we are entirely lost and must call a Mayday on the yacht's radio to get help!

Now, let's consider taking an alternative voyage, going to the same destination as before; where, this time, we also take into consideration the influence and behaviours of the variable winds and tides on our actual direction of travel and continuously make small adjustments to our bearing by marking our progress at regular times on the chart, and thereby steering the boat by a consistently updated compass heading towards Le Havre.

We do not all have to be seasoned sailors to understand the difference between these two approaches. The first is to focus too rigidly on a fixed heading or a direction of travel and thereby miss the ultimate destination, which could, potentially, lead to a disaster.

The second is to make the destination the focus, and then adapt our direction of travel concerning any external shifts in behaviour, tailoring our journey to suit whatever the environment or situation throws at us.

Stakeholder engagement is just like this. It is about ensuring that our focus is on the destination and not the direction of travel. In other words, it is about enabling our stakeholders and not disabling them through the relentless pursuit of any of our singular objectives and, thereby, ensuring that we both enjoy a mutually beneficial journey towards an agreed outcome.

Imagine just how powerful it would be if we set a course towards a destination of *'delighting'* every single one of our stakeholders.

When we refer back to making each stakeholder interaction about *them* and not about *us,* and we combine this with a genuine wish to ultimately *delight* them, we begin to realise the necessity to spend a great deal more time to really get to know and understand each of our stakeholders' unique requirements.

Activity

Detail how you might set a new destination for each of your stakeholders. Decide on your initial 'heading' and then be prepared to flex your approach to suit changes in environmental or stakeholder behaviours.

chapter 8

———

Developing others

What is it?

The developing others dimension regards a human activity that we each do from time to time; as a parent, a friend, a manager or, for some, as a professional trainer or coach.

Developing people in terms of emotional intelligence is not just about sharing our expertise or knowledge with them. It is more profound, in as much as we each need to fully comprehend the people themselves before we may be privileged enough to be a part of their development process.

The developing others dimension covers:

- Understanding others
- Developing individuals
- Coaching skills

Your dimension feedback

Use the *average* score that you recorded for this particular PEIP dimension to review the relevant feedback, as detailed by the corresponding levels of 1 to 6 below.

Level 1: Incomprehensive – Uninvolved – Disinterested

You may lack the emotional connection with people to gain an understanding of their particular development requirements; this will lead to you either not getting involved in their development at all or possibly a lack of interest in the subject. Unfortunately, it is most likely that your approach to people development will be uninspiring.

Level 2: Telling – Instructing – Teaching

You like to tell people what to do, you instruct them on the rights and wrongs of a situation. You feel comfortable when teaching people within your areas of expertise or interest. The problem with this command-and-control approach is that the listener often perceives this as one-way communication and is likely to become quickly disinterested or disenchanted with the subject matter.

Level 3: Listening – Supporting – Growing

You listen well to what people have to say before you advise them on their best course of action and then support them through the change. While this may serve some people in some situations, it will not always encourage the learning that will help them grow. People learn through doing and not just through listening.

Level 4: Engaging – Guiding – Mentoring

You take time to understand people well; you listen, engage them thoroughly and then guide them towards the right outcome for them in their situation. While this might be extremely useful and beneficial in many cases, providing a mentoring facility is about sharing your expertise and is, therefore, not entirely focused on them developing their capabilities.

Level 5: Solutions – Enabling – Coaching

You elegantly coach people to find and reach solutions to their problems by using active listening and practical open questioning skills, enabling them to define the pathway for their learning and development as well as guiding them towards better outcomes.

Level 6: Consulting – Empowering – Inspiring

You take the process of coaching up to the next level through using inspirational conversation techniques, combined with powerful open questioning and using a well-honed consultative approach; you empower people to flourish, develop and grow towards achieving their goals.

Developing your EI in this dimension

Understanding others

Delving into the complexities of human nature before we have a solid understanding of ourselves is likely to be a little more than just tricky. Let's face it, we have enough trouble understanding the thought processes going on inside our heads, let alone the thousands of impulses likely to be emerging and then flying around in other people's heads!

When we combine those impulses with the complications of language, attitude and physical behaviours, and then overlay these with such things as inclination, disposition, attitude, personality or individual preferences, we can only then begin to understand the many challenges that we face.

We are all different!

Suppose that we start from this singular premise in terms of understanding others, we are then less likely to make those *assumptions* that might preclude us from gaining accurate knowledge and, thereby, a realistic understanding of them.

It is all too frequently more comfortable for us to group another under a person, behaviour, or personality *type*, rather than getting to understand them as unique individuals. Yet, we all do it. We bunch together the limited information we have ascertained from what we have seen, heard or felt and immediately consign that information, inside our heads, to a *type* of person.

This is human nature; probably another leftover flaw within our outdated *tribal* mentality, where we feel the need to rationalise a person into a category that we may personally relate to or not. The problem with this obsolete thinking modality is that there is likely to be some *hidden potential,* the significant grey area between whatever black and white mental imprints we have determined as a type A or type B person.

Geshe Michael Roach and Lama Christie McNally, in their excellent book *The Diamond Cutter*, explain *hidden potential*:

> 'We have seen first of all that everything has a hidden potential, a kind of fluidity about what it could be. No person we meet is irritating from their own side, because there's always someone there who finds them quite charming; no matter how they seem to us, it's not something that's coming from them. So where's it coming from? Obviously, it's somehow coming from us, from our own minds.'

Instead of assuming anything about another person, if we were to seek the *hidden potential* within them, we might just begin to realise the authentic potential hidden within ourselves!

I wrote in the previous chapter about the differences between an assumption and a perception. What we now need to consider is ensuring that those perceptions are qualified and remain still valid.

The only way of checking our perceptions is through detailed enquiry. And that means getting to know the other person for themselves and not for ourselves. To do this, we need to challenge our perceptions; we need to determine if those perceptions would have the validity that would stand up, even if we were in a court of law.

It is not that difficult to do if we are genuinely enthusiastic about really wanting to get to understand others and their hidden potential more. We all know what it feels like when people ask us those bland questions only then to appear utterly disinterested in our answers.

To fully gain an understanding of others, we need to engage in proper conversation, the to-and-fro of *real dialogue*! As any successful person will attest, this often means listening a lot more than speaking. Which also means making the conversation about them, and not always about us!

Being curious about others simply requires asking open questions and listening to their answers thoroughly before asking another question that, ideally, is related to that answer.

It should be straightforward, yet, for some of us, it can become challenging, especially if we are too focused on trying to steer the conversation towards our objectives and not theirs.

Activity

Identify a person whom you know reasonably well and then set out on a journey of discovery to discover their *hidden potential* through engaging with them using an open question dialogue. An example of the type of question route you could use initially might be:

1 What specifically do you enjoy about your current role?
   And, then, based on their answer:

> **2** In what way are those particular aspects of your role important?
> *And, then, based on their answer:*
>
> **3** How might you use these specific aspects to help you further?
> *And, then, based on their answer . . .*

Developing individuals

We do not all need to be qualified trainers to develop other people, far from it. Some of the best training I have ever had has come from friends, family, colleagues, or my boss and none of them had anything more than a reasonable level of mastery in that particular area.

The best advice for anyone looking to develop another is to take the role of a facilitator or, if we prefer, what someone once described to me as a 'guide on the side' rather than the 'sage on the stage'.

By removing ourselves directly from being at the centre of the learner's attention, we enable them to focus on the task and the learning itself, rather than on us. We can then help guide them through to completion of any duty or activity by using open questions and supportive dialogue wherever possible.

Make it about 'them' – I know that I say this an awful lot. However, when it comes to being emotionally intelligent, that is the point; we cannot be emotionally intelligent if we only focus on ourselves.

Gone are the days of telling. We know from experience that, unless the teller has an incredible monologue performance ability, which might hold our attention long enough for them to get the learning across, we are more likely to find other more exciting things to focus our attention on.

We know for a fact that people learn much faster through trial and error than they do through instruction, yet we still fall back into the preach and teach mentality.

Children would never learn to walk if we simply told them how to do it. They must experience it for themselves, and that means developing the neural pathways within their brains that will ensure that they gain balance as well as transmitting the right impulses to the right muscle groups at the right time.

Throughout our lives, the process of learning does not change. When we learn something new, neural pathways become established and, once these pathways have been tried and tested through practice, they evolve from being a conscious thought to becoming a subconscious process.

An example of this might be when we learn to drive a motor vehicle. To start learning, we must actively think, consciously, about each activity, like mirror, signal and manoeuvre. Yet, after driving for a while, we seldom need to think about these now 'subconscious' behaviours or processes.

The problem only comes along when we need to unlearn something in order to learn or re-learn something else, which is not the same as just deleting a file on our computer and replacing it with a new one.

We must switch the neural pathways inside our heads, which are often running concurrently; the older learnt behaviours may already have evolved into subconscious processes, while the new paths will still be in our conscious learning thought processes.

As many schoolteachers will attest, how we learn is also based on a simple model of challenge vs skills. If the 'challenge' is low, while the skills are high, the brain gets bored and frustrated. If the 'challenge' is high, and the 'skill' is low, then the brain becomes stressed.

Always remember that, just because we have managed to master a skill quickly, it does not necessarily mean that it is also easy for someone else who may not have the same mental or physical dexterity as ourselves.

The best way of learning is to ensure that there is an equal balance of challenge and skill involved, which, like the diagram below demonstrates, can ultimately become a state of flow. This also serves to describe potential situations where, through deliberately becoming aware of learners' different behaviours, we can identify when they are experiencing each of the various shifts in emotional states.

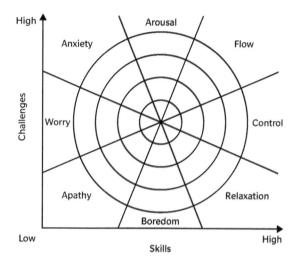

Activity

Think of how you like to learn a new task and relate this to the emotional states as detailed in the diagram.

1 What might you learn by effectively balancing *challenge* with *skill*?

2 What might you consciously have to do differently?

3 How might this help you learn faster or better in the future?

Coaching skills

One of the very best coaches I ever encountered was while I was travelling to London on a train. I was sitting in a busy carriage opposite a young mother and her five-year-old daughter.

The daughter, we shall call her Annabel, was sitting in the window seat and colouring in a picture of Santa Claus, and the conversation went something like this:

Mother: 'Annabel, that is a beautiful picture. Who is the main person in it?'

Annabel: 'Oh, that's Santa Claus.'

Mother: 'And what is Santa Claus doing?'

Annabel: 'He is learning to write.'

Mother: 'How do you know that he is learning to write?'

Annabel: 'Because he is using the wrong hand to hold his pen.'

Mother: 'Which hand is he using to write with?'

Annabel: 'He is using his right hand.'

Mother: 'Which hand should he be using?'

Annabel: 'He should be using his left hand, like me.'

Mother: 'Oh, I see, and which hand do I use to write with?'

Annabel: 'Hmm, you write with your other hand.'

Mother: 'Why do I write with my right hand?'

Annabel: 'Hmm, because you like your right hand more.'

Mother: 'Which hand do you think Santa Claus likes?'

Annabel: 'Hmm, Santa Claus likes his right hand more too.'

Mother: 'What do you think that Santa Claus is writing?'

Annabel: 'He is writing a book for left-handed people!'

Simple, elegant and an excellent example of great coaching. The mother could so easily have told Annabel about left and right-handed preferences, yet she wanted Annabel to understand it and work it out for herself.

That pretty much sums up what coaching others is. Coaching is the art of asking open questions that enable the other person to find the right solution or answer themselves.

If we go into a coaching conversation, having already determined an outcome and then try to manipulate the other person towards it, that is not coaching!

Coaching others is a collaborative process where we use questions and their answers to help them create an internal frame of reference towards a potentially different way of doing or understanding things.

The reason why coaching works so much better than simple instruction is down to our physical neurology. As previously stated, new pathways need to be established and tested in our brains before they finally become embedded in our subconscious.

We can't create those new pathways externally; they must be self-induced and relevant to our existing thought process or, at the very least, they will become relevant after practice and experience.

If we intend to have a coaching conversation, it is always good advice to ensure that there is adequate time for the session to conclude. There is nothing worse than having to finish off at another time, where the essential threads of the conversation have become obsolete.

Pay attention to the physical environment. While our office may seem very comfortable for us, it may feel inhibiting to someone else to be sitting on the other side of our desk looking at us.

Many coaches recommend sitting near the other person, maybe at a 45-degree angle, although sitting alongside someone at their desk may be just as useful.

A stroll in a park away from the office environment might be more beneficial than a forced conversation in a meeting room. I have even suggested to a coachee that we go out for a drive in a car, where we can then find a quiet (neutral) location to sit comfortably and talk.

There is no right and wrong location. It is all about making sure that both parties feel comfortable and allows for an uninterrupted flow of dialogue.

Do not judge them. We can't be coaching if we are judging. If we believe that something is right or wrong, we may end up forcing our opinions unnecessarily. It is far better to withhold our beliefs and to explore theirs instead.

We need to ensure that the coaching conversation is as fluid as possible. Use open questions. The logical levels of questioning I detail in the section on 'Questioning' in Chapter 11 is a good starting point; it does not mean, however, that we need to create a rigid framework from which to work.

Reaching a logical conclusion at each stage by enabling the other person to articulate a summary of the conversation to that point is always a good move, better still is ensuring that they have an action plan to navigate their way forward.

Some examples of questions to include to help this along the way might be:

- 'What do you need to do differently to ensure that this happens?'
- 'How might you ensure that this is going to work?'
- 'Who can you liaise with to get this working?'
- 'When will you do this by?'
- 'How might you ensure that you stay on track?'
- 'How do you feel about this new course of action?'
- 'What is essential for you to do next?'

Activity

Using the information from this chapter and using the headings detailed below, create an outline for a personal development plan for a person to follow. They could be a member of your work team or your home team, an employee, colleague, friend or family member. It might even be a plan for your development.

Personal development plan

Suggested headings might include:

1 Set the objective – define the goal in as much detail as possible.

2 What are their current strengths?

3 Describe what *perceived* developmental areas might be required – and how you might then determine these to be accurate.

4 What skills or knowledge gaps may exist?

5 Create actions – when, where, how and, possibly, why.

6 Identify realistic time frames.

7 How, specifically, will you track progress by incorporating regular and timely reviews?

chapter 9

Developing empathy

What is it?

The empathy dimension is about our ability to identify, read, comprehend and share the feelings of other people.

The empathy dimension covers:

- Respect
- Rapport
- Adaptive behaviour

Your dimension feedback

Use the *average* score that you recorded for this particular PEIP dimension to review the relevant feedback, as detailed by the corresponding levels of 1 to 6 below.

Level 1: Disrespectful – Disagreement – Inflexible

The level of disinterest or apathy that you demonstrate towards other people, combined with your inflexibility towards them, may well encourage disagreement and lack of commitment towards your ideas or suggestions.

Level 2: Opinionated – Antagonistic – Condescending

Through your opinionated and, thereby, potentially conde-scending approach towards others, you will, inevitably, find that there is always likely to be an antagonistic air surrounding you. People may prefer to keep clear of you, which might be why you feel the need to disassociate from them in the first place.

Level 3: Acknowledgement – Comfort – Compassion

You build a certain level of accord with people, through acknowledging their strengths, being comfortable engaging with them and through developing a level of compassion with them. However, this comes with, perhaps, a little too much internal focus and not enough external attention.

Level 4: Value – Mirror – Adapt

You quickly establish rapport with people because you value them as people, you are comfortable mirroring their communication style and, most importantly, you will adapt your style to suit them.

Level 5: Respect – Engaging – Flexibility

You demonstrate a natural affinity with people, you comfort-ably engender and show respect to them, you create flexible and joined-up approaches to solving problems and encourage them to excel at what they do.

Level 6: Humble – Intuitive – Synergy

You create harmonious relationships because you remain very humble in your approach to other people. Through allowing your intuition to guide and shape the context of the communication, you inevitably create a synergistic environment for others to flourish.

Developing your EI in this dimension

Respect

When I was growing up, my mother used to remind me that, 'It is not what you say, but the way you say it,' that matters most.

While I still agree with this principle, I think that, in the days of modern communication, we need to be thinking more about the actual words we use, as well as the way we use them.

Don't think about the number nine!

So, why did you think about it?

The simple answer might be that our subconscious brains do not recognise the word don't, though we all understand the concept of don't. If we are doing something and another person says, 'Don't do that,' we will stop or, at the very least, ask why.

Yet, by linking don't with a different set of instructions, it can become autosuggestion. Imagine saying, 'Don't be stupid,' to a seven-year-old boy every time that he made a small mistake and, if we continued to say this, day in and day out, over several years, what do you think would happen to him by the time he reached his early teens?

Is he more likely to become highly capable, or will he just think that he is stupid?

Unfortunately, the most significant likelihood is that he will have low levels of self-esteem, a general lack of confidence and, possibly yes, even though perhaps capable, he might believe that he is stupid.

Yet, I am amazed at how many parents, and even teachers, use negative words when trying to educate and develop their young people. Imagine, that rather than saying, 'Don't be stupid,' the parent or teacher used phrases such as: 'Be clever,' 'Use your brain,' or even, 'Be wise.'

What do we think the likelihood is of the boy becoming a more rounded, confident and far more capable teenager if he was subjected to more 'enabling' rather than 'disabling' communication during his upbringing?

Let's think back to our own childhood: were all the words that helped shape us deliberately positive, emotionally grounded and fully intent on helping us to flourish and grow?

I have to say that, if they were, unfortunately, we would be in a small minority of the entire world's population. We are all guilty of poor communication, even within our own families!

I have spent most of my life working with adults who are the result of their early conditioning, which has also played an essential part in shaping their future selves. In more cases than you might imagine, this has resulted in them having lower levels of self-esteem and outward confidence.

When we choose the right words to use at the right time and place, we are demonstrating respect for others' rights, feelings and wishes. Gone are the days of, *'Respect should be well earned.'* Respect should be implicit. It should be the foundation for each communication we have with one another, yet, sadly, it is not always the case.

We can so easily disrespect another person by the words we use, the tone or inclination of our voice, the assumptions we have made about them or, indeed, the imperfect reality we have created about them within our minds.

The adage of: *'While I may disagree with what you say, I fully respect your reasons for saying it'* is the right way of thinking about respect as an attitude. Showing respect is about showing acceptance, allowing the other person to have their voice, irrespective of any difference in opinion we may hold.

Activity

Around 1875, the English writer Lewis Carroll wrote a nonsense poem called *The Hunting of The Snark*. The Snark was a mythical creature, probably based on another earlier nonsense work of his called *Jabberwocky*. The Jabberwocky character, incidentally, was also portrayed later in *Alice Through the Looking Glass* or better known as *Alice in Wonderland*.

On a blank sheet of paper, and then using only a pencil or pen, I would like you to define and then design a *Snark!*

Say the word *Snark* out loud, then let your imagination run riot, have some fun; there are no bad ideas; just create your version of a *Snark* and draw what your *Snark* will look like on your piece of paper.

Have you done it?

Unfortunately, I can't see your drawing, although I do know, from running this same exercise with groups, that, in 85 per cent of cases, delegates choose to create their mythical creature based on the sound that the word makes.

Usually, the result is not a pleasant creature; it is often spiky, has sharp teeth and, otentially, is quite a vicious-looking animal.

Why do you think that is?

The reason for this is based on two types of conditioning; the first is that the word *Snark* is a 'spiky' word. It sounds harsh, probably because of the k at the end of the name.

And the second relates to the symbolism of the two combined words of snake and shark, that already have inherent meaning for us deep within our subconscious minds and are both often perceived as hazardous.

Whereas a few people, 15 per cent, don't view the name as spiky or maybe don't have the earlier conditioning of snakes or sharks being as dangerous and are, therefore, more likely to choose creatures that may appear softer or kinder.

Was I deliberately trying to influence you when I wrote the exercise? Take a look back and look at how I wrote it and think about how that may have affected the decision-making process you used.

Was I respectful to you in that situation? Probably not, although I would not want you to think wrong of me. I just wanted to show you how easy it is for us to influence and then, possibly, through that influence, disrespect others with the words we choose to use.

Every day, we say and do things without any pre-thought or, worse still, with pre-thought of using particular words to elicit an appropriate or inappropriate response that would, more likely, be in our favour!

Let's now return to the subject of types of positive or negative words and phrases that we use daily. The following grid represents *the six levels of emotional efficacy*, which we covered in Chapter 5; it will help you to gain a better understanding of how our language or, more precisely, the words we use, affects our level of emotional efficacy.

Note: this grid is by no means a definitive list of words under each level or heading. Although it might appear a little contrived at first, it does serve to outline the difference that words make when related to a particular 'people-centric' level.

Indication of typical word usage across the 'six levels of emotional efficacy'

Level:	1	2	3	4	5	6
Name:	Against	Despite	With	Harmony	Empower	Mastery
Centric intention	I	You	We	Us	They	All
The words typically used at each level:	Don't	Will	Can	Team	Do	Be
	Can't	Not	Shall	Give	Encourage	Unity
	Shan't	Must	Have	Help	Enable	Others
	Won't	Tell	Will	Share	Enjoin	Always
	Deny	Mistake	May	Exchange	Entrust	Selfless
	Never	Lousy	Maybe	Create	Options	Open
	Not	Poor	Do	Nurture	Possibility	Shared
	Restrict	Deny	Permit	Enable	Delegate	Warrant
	Negate	Reject	Allow	Empathise	Opinions	Caring
	Fail	Terrible	Good	Engage	Create	Kind
	Bad	Stupid	Clever	Encourage	Valued	Respect
	No, but	Yes, but	Yes, and	Yes, and let's	Yes, how will we?	Yes?

Activity

Think of the specific words that you tend to use the most and consider how these might induce the right or wrong negative state of emotions in other people.

> An example may be if you are prone to use the words 'Yes, but' at the beginning of a sentence, it may cause the other person to think that you doubt them or their integrity.
>
> Now answer the following questions:
>
> - According to the grid, at what level are most of the words you currently use?
>
> - How does this compare to your PEIP assessment?
>
> - What words will you try to avoid using in future, and why should you refrain from using them?
>
> - How might you measure and review these changes?
>
> - What words do you need to focus on to maintain a positive state across all of your interactions?

Rapport

I rather like the idea that rapport is the synergistic entity between two or more people that enables the seemingly effortless transfer of information and knowledge.

Although this may seem a lot to get our heads around initially, being in genuine rapport with another human being is one of life's greatest pleasures and gifts. It stimulates our head and our hearts; it splendidly combines our emotional and rational neurological processes.

When we are in rapport, we're consciously and subconsciously engaged. All our emotional senses are heightened, to the point that we may very well be 'subconsciously' mirroring many physical aspects of the other person.

A great example of this is when we are, perhaps, sitting in a bar or a restaurant in deep conversation with a friend or colleague, totally unaware that we are entirely copying them.

We adopt similar postures; we use the same tone of voice. We might pick our drinks up at the same time, we might smile or laugh instantaneously and, if we chose to focus enough, we might also find that we are breathing at the same rate and, possibly, even, blinking at the same time!

It's a little weird when we first consciously notice the mirroring effect happening to ourselves and others. I am pretty sure that we can attribute these mirroring functions for developing rapport to the same sense of 'tribe' that we discussed in Chapter 6.

We all like to be liked, and we become more liked by being just like the other person!

Observe any small child in a social setting for long enough, and we begin to see them subtly mirroring the adults around them. That's how they learn about social interaction, by subconsciously copying the movements, facial expressions, gestures and, sometimes, the words of others.

Those new, often subtle, behaviours get processed in the neocortex part of the brain. After a while, we might try them out for ourselves and then further hone or disregard them entirely.

Like all other learning, when we perceive those new behaviours or expressions relevant to us, they become embedded in our subconscious mind. They then form part of our subconscious reactions during social interaction going forward.

Because these social behaviours are often so very subtle, they can easily be misinterpreted by us and, thereby, possibly lead to the wrong responses!

Building rapport consciously and deliberately through mirroring is a skill that has been practised by many highly successful leaders, managers, HR, salespeople and many other people-focused people for decades.

Some find the idea of consciously mirroring deliberately a little challenging, even though subconscious mirroring is an entirely natural thing for them to do.

To make this easier, we could think about it as relearning to ride a bike, after several years out of the saddle. Sure enough, we will make some small mistakes at first, although, once the neural pathways have been fully reconnected, we will be gliding along in no time at all.

Another great way of building rapport is to imagine ourselves in their position while we are talking with them. We might want to notice their current posture and why they may have adopted that position or stance.

Pay attention to their language and even try to listen to the space between the words they use, as this will help us to tune in to them more as a person and ensure that we remain deliberately in time with them.

Becoming curious about them as an individual will help focus our dialogue towards them and not towards ourself.

Building rapport should feel effortless to both parties. If it does not, then we may very well be trying too hard and it may appear to the other person that we are trying to become their new best friend!

Give building rapport sufficient time as it does not always happen immediately. Remember to relax and smile, be yourself, be genuine and authentic and, before too long, you will have established a similar response from the other person.

Activity

The next time you are involved in a deep conversation, deliberately become more conscious of the other person.

Watch how they might start to mirror the way you are sitting, moving or gesturing.

Tune into their movements and tone, pitch and speed of their voice and then, at an appropriate time in the conversation, gently nod your head in agreement with them and watch to see if they start to mirror you.

Adaptive behaviour

In terms of emotional intelligence, enabling ourselves and others to become fully engaged within our environment to pursue the greatest success and the least conflict is what adaptive behaviour is all about.

How many times a day do we find ourselves and others not adapting our behaviours to suit the environment, let alone towards all the people within it?

The answer is far too often! We are all guilty of following routines, of rightly or wrongly adhering to those preferences or beliefs that we have created in our minds about how things should be and, subsequently, not being prepared to flex our behaviours enough when challenged.

Let us first explore why we may have, inadvertently, established some of those preferences and see if we can unpick any of them to help us adapt our behaviour.

Richard Bandler and John Grinder, the creators of NLP (neuro-linguistic programming) in the 1970s, identified a model based on our 'representational systems' that indicates that we have a predisposed way of processing information based on our preferred sensory perspectives.

- *Visual people* will prefer to use visually related language contexts, such as: what they see, how they describe things through
  colours or images through patterns, how they might use visual
  words like appear, view, focus, imagine, watch, bright, open or
  transparent.

- *Auditory people* will prefer to use auditory-related language contexts, such as: what they have heard, how something may sound
  to them, and they may use auditory words like listen, hear, mention, inquire, discuss, sound, tune in, vocal, say, remark.

- *Kinaesthetic people* will prefer to use kinaesthetic-related language contexts, such as: how they feel about things, and they may
  use words like feel, touch, robust, weak, impression, hot, cold,
  relaxed, enforced.

There is another element to representational systems called *kinaesthetic dialogue,* which deals with our internal logic and the method
we use to talk to ourselves around the sense that we make of things.

Although relevant, we shall concentrate on the three sensory perspectives being: visual, auditory and kinaesthetic (VAK) for short.
We will, for this purpose, combine both physical and sensory feelings under K for kinaesthetic.

The words that people use daily are a pretty accurate reflection
of their preferred sense. If someone says, 'I *see* what you mean,' for
example, there is a pretty high chance that they have a preferred
visual internal representation of the world.

Likewise, if someone says, 'It *sounds* like we might need to do something else,' that will, most likely, indicate that they have a preferred auditory internal representation of the world.

Whereas, if someone says, 'I *feel* as though we should do something,' there is an equally high chance that they will have more of an internal kinaesthetic representation of the world.

The reason why we might need to identify these variances in others is so that we can adapt our own language to suit them, rather than just sticking with our personal preference.

Imagine a conversation that might occur where one party is using a different preference to the other party, and we may well understand why so many communications fail.

Here is a typical business conversation where this could happen:

John: 'Hello, Sam, I *hear* that there has been a problem with your order.'

Sam: 'Yes, that's right, John. It doesn't *look* like you have the stock I require.'

John: '*Sounds* to me like you may have input the wrong information when ordering because we aren't short of any of our main products.'

Sam: 'I *see*. Well, I did double-check the order numbers against the catalogue, and it *looked* fine to me.'

John: '*Listen*, Sam. If you had put the right numbers in, then we would not have a problem now, would we?'

Sam: 'If you *view* the order I sent in and check it against your catalogue, you will *see* that everything fits.'

John: 'I'll *mention* it to the guys in the order fulfilment team and come back to you shortly with their *answer*.'

I am sure you get the idea about just how awkward this conversation was beginning to *feel*. It certainly did not represent excellent customer service. So, let's rerun it with John *verbally mirroring* Sam and see what happens.

John: 'Hello, Sam. I *see* we have a problem with your order.'

Sam: 'Yes, that's right, John. It doesn't *look* like you have the stock I require.'

John: '*Looks* to me like you may have input the wrong information when ordering because we are not short of any of our main products.'

Sam: 'I *see*. Well, I did double-check the order numbers against the catalogue, and it *looked* fine to me.'

John: 'Let's take a *look* at what you ordered.'

Sam: 'If you *view* the order I sent in and check it against your catalogue, you will see that everything fits.'

John: 'Yes, you are right; it does *look* OK. I will share this with the guys in order fulfilment and come back to you shortly with their point of *view* and, hopefully, we will *see* how we can resolve this.'

Similar conversation, yet, the second time, it flowed more effortlessly towards a potential outcome to ensure that the customer was kept onside and happy.

Eye accessing cues is another way of potentially identifying a person's representational preference. Although not a proven scientific fact, the theory still works in practice; that, when we are thinking about a subject matter using any one of our preferred representation systems, our eyes will move towards a specific location.

The following image identifies how this works and, as you will notice, is based on a right-handed person. A left-hander will, sometimes, although not always, be opposite in terms of their past and future perspectives.

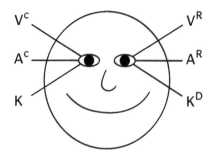

Visual accessing cues for 'normally organised' right-handed person
V^C = visually constructed, V^R = visually remembered (eyes focused up and unmoving = visual accessing); A^C = auditory constructed, A^R = auditory remembered (eyes centrally focused and unmoving = auditory accessing); K = kinaesthic, K^D = kinaesthetic dialogue (eyes focused down and unmoving = kinaesthetic accessing).

It is also worthwhile remembering that we can all use each of these preferences, at various times and in different environments, to access further information in our heads, irrespective of our favoured method.

Activity

Using this model, think about your preference. It might help for you to notice where your eyes go when you answer the following question out loud:
'Where did you grow up?'

There is a very high chance that your eyes went top, middle or bottom towards your left or your right. Whichever side it was will denote your *past* preferences, and the opposite side will be your future preference.

Whether your eyes went to the top, middle or the bottom will also help you identify your preference in terms of being more visual, auditory or kinaesthetic.

chapter 10

Developing credibility

What is it?

The credibility dimension comprises both the objective components, such as knowledge and skill, as well as subjective components of honesty, reliability, attitude and capability.

The credibility dimension covers:

- Integrity
- Capability
- Knowledge

Your dimension feedback

Use the *average* score that you recorded for this particular PEIP dimension to review the relevant feedback, as detailed by the corresponding levels of 1 to 6 below.

Level 1: Dishonest – Unskilled – Uncertain

Your lack of a moral perspective is likely to engender a feeling of dishonesty from others. Combine this with feelings of limited capability and you may not be surprised why others may regard you with a level of uncertainty or a lack of clarity.

Level 2: Divisive – Unrealistic – Improbable

You are very likely to be perceived as being 'divisive' if the level of your integrity fluctuates too much against any unrealistic stated capabilities; this will, undoubtedly, leave people feeling that your overall credibility is 'improbable'.

Level 3: Honourable – Able – Knowledgeable

Your credibility is 'tenable'. What this means is that, although you demonstrate a healthy level of integrity and are, undoubtedly, knowledgeable, there may well be some concerns over your capability due to the level of confidence you display in particular situations.

Level 4: Integrity – Capability – Reliable

Although you demonstrate integrity, you have the right capability and you can be relied upon to get the job done. The only element that might be missing for you is a strong enough belief in yourself; this may give rise to others perceiving your credibility as 'laudable'.

Level 5: Honesty – Professional – Curiosity

The level of your credibility is 'dependable'. You demonstrate a high level of honesty; you are professional in your dealings with other people. You are curious about finding new ways to improve and develop yourself and others.

Level 6: Dependable – Humble – Expert

You are an 'authentic' person; people find it easy to depend on you due to your considerable expertise delivered in a quiet, unassuming, even humble way.

Developing your EI in this dimension

Integrity

There are two meanings for integrity; the first is about being honest with strong moral principles, and the second is regarding a state of being as a whole or undivided.

I believe that we need to combine both meanings and relate them directly to our internal and external emotional points of reference, ensuring that we maintain a consistent approach across every part of our lives.

The big problem with this is that life gets in the way; we must make compromises and, sometimes, those compromises will challenge our integrity. Consider a situation where, perhaps, you might be looking to sell your house and upgrade to another type of property. You have already found the ideal property to buy, in the right location and at an excellent price.

The estate agent comes to value your existing property and, as you are walking around with him, he asks you about your neighbours.

The problem you have is that you do not like your neighbours; they have been rude and aggressive towards you; they are very noisy. They think nothing of having loud music playing all night long, especially in the summer months when they are entertaining outside almost every evening.

How might you answer the estate agent with integrity?

Some people may be comfortable compromising their integrity if a particular outcome is likely to have a direct effect on any financial or career opportunity. It is just business, after all!

Similar types of random integrity challenges pop up across all areas of our lives, and it is how we deal with them, using our integrity, that determines the right emotionally intelligent outcome for us.

I often experience the problems faced by people who have been in a typical situation, where, through no fault of their own, they have ended up working for a boss, or a whole organisation of people, whose integrity is suspect. And, where the individual concerned is no longer comfortable operating outside the moral framework of their beliefs or values.

My advice is always that the problem with making any compromise in our integrity is that it will, unquestionably, lead to feelings of ill-will, by one or more of the parties concerned.

A short story that I remember from my childhood was when an old farmer called all his 10 children together and said that, in order to decide on which one of them would inherit the farm, he was going to set them a challenge.

He gave them each a single seed of corn and told them to plant it in a pot and nurture it for 100 days. The child who gained the best result would inherit the farm.

All the children planted their seeds and, before very long, all except one of the pots had little shoots growing in them. The one that did not have a shoot belonged to a daughter called Isabella and, although she watered and tended the pot daily, by the end of 100 days, she still did not have a plant to show her father.

When all her brothers brought their successful fully grown corn to be judged by their father, they laughed at poor Isabella's empty pot.

Their father immediately, though, decided that Isabella would inherit the farm because he had secretly boiled each of the seeds, which would stop any growth before he had given them to his children.

Integrity is, after all, our moral compass. No matter how hard the challenges within our lives, it should always guide our words, actions and thoughts.

Activity

1 Think of your opinion of someone with integrity whom you admire:

- What do they do specifically?
- How do they display their integrity?
- What does their integrity sound like?
- How does their integrity make you feel?

2 Now, consider your opinion for someone whom you believe has limited or no integrity and ask yourself the same four questions.

If you perceive that any part of your integrity is not as substantial as it should be, then it might be time for you to put a plan in place that will help you address this and ensure that other people do not have similar answers to your opinions in no. 2, above.

Capability

'Capability is the ability to do things and to choose for a way of life according to one's values.

As it applies to human capital, capability represents performing or achieving certain actions/outcomes in terms of the intersection of capacity and ability.'

I like the first part of this description of capability most because it helps challenge us to define *capability* as a *choice* and a way of life, plus it also links it directly to our values.

Capability helps us to determine our internal permissions and limitations; it describes what we know and what we can or can't do. It incorporates our personal blueprint in defining us as unique individuals by demonstrating *what* we can do, as well as *how* we are most likely to do it.

We each build capability relative to our life's situation at that time. What changes from one individual to another are the drivers or reasons for that capability to take place.

The more powerful the driver, the more impact there will be in our ability to attain additional capability quickly and effectively. When those drivers are further influenced by a direct correlation with our values and beliefs, they may even become 'supercharged'!

Consider a situation where an individual is in an unsuitable role and, by 'unsuitable', I make the differentiation between a position aligned with the individual's values and beliefs as opposed to lacking the essential skills or knowledge needed to fulfil the requirements of the job.

Interesting thought, isn't it?

Many people may have the essential skills to perform a task. Yet, their capability to deliver it exceptionally well will be governed by their values and beliefs, which then determines the individual choices they make.

I know from personal experience just how tiresome it becomes trying to do something when my heart (emotional intelligence) is not in it. In other words, when I do something that is not linked directly to my personal choices or preferences (based on my beliefs and values), I lack the motivation, the curiosity or even the will to engage fully with the subject matter.

Time and again, as a management/leadership trainer, I came across the same situation where delegates turned up for a training course because someone else had booked them onto it. And, if the workshop was not their choice, they had already, mentally, checked out of the training room, even before the beginning of day one.

We can all read material to develop our ability. Yet, we need to make a conscious choice to incorporate that new knowledge into our lives and then, only through choosing to practise and build experience, will we be able to define our capability in that field.

Building our capability must be a personal choice, and those choices will change continuously across our lives. Yet, our more consistent values and beliefs should enable the choices we make through those times.

Identifying your preferences

Only once you have identified each value and how it shapes your beliefs and behaviours, can you then consider how these have influenced the choices you make, which enable or inhibit your capability.

To consider this further, I have detailed below an adaptation of the Logical Levels of Change model created by Robert Dilts in the 1970s, which was, as it happens, based on an earlier work of scientist and philosopher Gregory Bateson.

If you are familiar with the Dilts model, you will notice that I have separated *beliefs* and *values,* as I feel these are separate entities unto themselves. For understanding EI, they should not be confused. Plus, I have replaced *purpose,* relating to the change model, with *self,* which I feel also ties it, although loosely, with Maslow's 'Hierarchy of Needs', a motivational theory used in psychology.

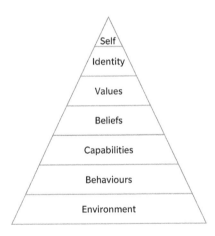

Starting from the bottom, we have:

- *Environment* – the environment level refers to everything outside of ourselves. This will, inevitably, include our home, work, the situations created by each of our stakeholders, the economy, even the current state of the world.

- *Behaviours* – at the next level, we can examine the specific practices or actions we take to satisfy the requirements of the environment at that time. The behaviour level is all about what we say and do. It is part of what is seen, heard and felt by other people.

- *Capabilities* – the next level involves the strategies, skills and knowledge by which we might marshal or select and direct behaviours relevant to that environment.

- *Beliefs* – our beliefs provide the reinforcement that supports or inhibits our capabilities and behaviours within the environment. Beliefs determine how events are given meaning and are at the core of both judgement and culture.

- *Values* – values are the criteria against which we make decisions. These criteria are qualities that we 'believe' to be important in the way we choose to live our lives and, thereby, give rise to our capabilities and the subsequent 'behaviours' we use for each 'environment' in which we find ourselves.

- *Identity* – our identity is the 'external' representation of ourselves. For it to be authentic, it must represent each of the previous levels.

- *Self* – self is about our subjective 'internal' experience of our identity, values, beliefs, capabilities and behaviours. In an ideal world, it should align beautifully with our 'external' reality and identity.

Activity

Using the adapted *Logical Levels* model, create a version of this, as large as you can, on a sheet of A4 paper, allowing enough space for you to write additional information within each level.

1 To start, we are going to focus on your *values*, by identifying a core trait or characteristic by which you choose to live your life. For example, this value might be something fundamentally important to you like honesty or integrity,

   If you are struggling with this, think a little broader by identifying a core value that people who know you well are most likely to say you possess.

2 Next, we are going to identify those *beliefs* that are a direct result of the value you have chosen. For example, if you chose honesty as your first value, then you may want to select words relating to your beliefs around honesty, such as *truth, openness, candour* or *morality*.

   Note: you will notice that the model has more space towards the bottom than it does the top. This additional space is deliberate; the further down in the model we go, the more attributes we need to have in support of the level above it and, likewise, the further up the model we go, the fewer the words become.

3 When you are happy with the words within *beliefs*, move down to *behaviours* to include those words that indicate how you carry out daily those behaviours, which are a direct result of those beliefs. For example, if you had *candour* in beliefs, your actions might be *frank, sincere, direct, fair, impartial* or *straightforward*.

4 Review the words you have chosen and then repeat the exercise with your next value, and keep going until you have built a clear picture of all the aspects that affect the choices you make and, thereby, the capability you bring.

   No two people will have the same number or even the same type of values. Do not get hung up on this aspect, write what is relevant and right for you at this point in your life.

Note: this is very important. And it is also going to be *big thinking stuff,* so do persevere, even if it means coming back to it over a few sessions.

Once you have completed this exercise, spend some more time focusing on how you can use this model and the information you have included as a useful springboard for adopting a 'whole of my life plan'.

You will be pleasantly surprised by the new direction your life might now start to take.

Knowledge

Philosophers have endeavoured to define what knowledge is precisely for many centuries. So, before we even begin to examine our awareness of this, from a perspective on emotional intelligence, let us first recall, in a brief summary, how Plato described knowledge, and whose doctrine is most likely to be as relevant today as it was in around 340 BC.

Plato described knowledge as a *justified, true belief.* In other words, to know something, it is justified as accurate. In contrast, a belief without proper justification or proof is merely a supposition.

We each remember essential information with varying levels of clarity; although, for some of us, particularly as we age, those levels of detail might become diminished in some way.

This decrease does not necessarily mean that the information is no longer there; it may just be a case of it no longer having as much importance to us as it first did.

In psychology, the conceptual term schema (or plural schemata) describes how our thoughts become organised through identifying the relationships, categories, relevance or patterns between them.

Schemata are said to develop from the correlation of all the information we gain throughout our life experiences. Our brains create schemata as a type of shortcut to make future encounters with similar situations or information more comfortable for us to navigate.

Schemata are likely to be reasonably rigid processes that are not able to adapt very quickly or particularly well to changing situations.

Schemata will influence the level of attention we give to a subject matter and how we may adopt or acquire new knowledge.

Let us suppose that something new does not fit or contradicts an existing schema. We may challenge or disregard the latest information or, in some rare situations, we might even distort the information to make it fit.

The key to enabling our schemata to operate efficiently is to ensure that we remain true to ourselves, our values and warrant that our beliefs are justified, based on some level of truth.

We also need to open our minds to new possibilities by removing any of the negative internal dialogue, which, as it also happens, is usually created by our unsupported beliefs, which then interfere with the potential of what that new knowledge might bring us.

Hidden knowledge

At some point in the past, we are likely to have heard someone say, 'Let me sleep on it,' when they have been unable to find an answer to conclude a particular situation or problem. And, nine times out of ten, after sleeping on it, they will find a relevant solution.

The reason why this happens to us is due to the small conscious *learning* part of the brain not being able to effectively tap into the much larger subconscious *already learnt* part of the brain at that time.

Even with an adequate level of mental health, this process is likely to be further influenced by time constraints, current commitments or other external pressures.

It may also be indicative of internal pressures, such as uncertainty, stress, anxiety or low confidence, which, by the way, if left unchecked, over a continued period, may lead to reduced levels of mental health.

If we refer back to the amygdala highjack, which we covered in Chapter 4, we begin to see similar brain functionality happening in other stressful situations.

Think of a nervous person walking onto a stage to engage a big audience, and it is not too difficult to imagine that, before long, they might freeze (just stand there), forget what they intend to say or stutter uncontrollably through their piece.

In times of stress, the limbic (emotional) system commandeers the rest of the brain to find the fastest solution. If it is unable to accomplish this, it is most likely to result in what some people may refer to as a partial or full mental block.

The solution, when mental blocks happen, is to temporarily step away from the situation, physically or, indeed, mentally. Once we do this, we are better able to find answers because we allow the focus within our minds to move from a reactive, cognitive thought process to a more relaxed and broader subconscious thought process.

That is great news, except when we are standing on a stage, and we have a few hundred people waiting expectantly for our words of wisdom. The last thing we feel we can realistically do is to step away from the situation.

What we can do, however, is take a few deep, slow (core) breaths, rest a second or two at the end of the last big breath and, if it is possible for us at the time, just explain to the audience that we are a little nervous in making our presentation in front of so many people.

This has two powerful effects; the first is it gives us time to calm our nerves and the second is that the majority of audiences are very understanding, especially if we are upfront and honest with them. We will always get the benefit of any doubt they may have if we proceed with total honesty and clarity.

The reason why this type of technique works, even for a hardened professional speaker like myself, is that, by becoming more humble in our whole approach, we inevitably encourage a lot more 'empathy' from the audience – remember: trust = empathy + credibility over the level of risk involved. If we do know our 'stuff', then we should have the credibility part all taken care of as well!

Here are eight tips you might like to help you uncover the hidden 'stuff' or knowledge and, also, they may assist you with any potential stage fright.

1 *Centre – Relax – Being light – Focus*: practise these techniques we talked about in Chapter 3. They will help you in all manner of situations requiring confidence.

2 Adopt your most natural, confident posture. Be yourself and make yourself comfortable. Whether standing or sitting, adopting a relaxed stance puts less stress on your body and brain.

3 Breathe slowly and deeply from your core.

4 Remove any negative internal dialogue and replace it with positive outcome-focused results, like visualising a delighted audience.

5 Be clear about your purpose and the value to your audience, moving your internal focus to them and not on you.

6 Connect with your audience, acknowledge them, make eye contact with them and remember to smile.

7 Be comfortable making mistakes, we all do it, and none of us is ever perfect.

8 Reduce your caffeine and sugar intake to reduce anxiety, especially during the two hours before you go on stage.

Activity

First – using the eight-point list above as a start, consider what other mental or physical techniques you might use to help steady your nerves or retrieve important information that you may be struggling to recall.

Next – think about the next time you are most likely to be in a situation where you may need to call on the hidden knowledge that you have. It does not have to be when you are making a presentation; it could be while you are on the phone, talking with a customer, in a meeting at work, or possibly even trying to solve a tricky issue at home.

Then – devise a simple mental strategy, maybe even using a mnemonic, a set of letters that form a single word to help you remember the elements, that you can call on when needed.

An example might be to use *'CRLF'* – Centre, Relax, Light and Focus, or something personal to yourself like *'BEING'* – Bright, Engaging, Interesting, Non-judgemental and Genuine.

Whatever you choose, make sure it is going to assist you entirely going forward, and have fun with it. The more silly it is, the more relaxed and lighter you will be when you need to call upon it.

chapter 11

Communication skills

What is it?

The communication dimension involves the transmission and the successful reception of any message by the intended recipient. Our emotional intelligence monitors how each element of the communication is devised and then processed, according to the relationship, beliefs, capabilities or any ambiguity that is present within a current situation.

The communication dimension covers:

- Style
- Listening
- Questioning

Your dimension feedback

Use the *average* score that you recorded for this particular PEIP dimension to review the relevant feedback, as detailed by the corresponding levels of 1 to 6 below.

Level 1: Inflexible – Ignores – Uninterested

Some may perceive your inflexible and uninterested approach to communication as being an ignore-ant. This behaviour typifies a 'Teenager' as it determines that point in our social development where we are still finding our identity, our way and likely to be unsure of our true capability.

Level 2: Unadaptive – Limited – Closed

We might describe this level of communication as being typical of a 'Politician', whereby you may appear to your audience as unadaptive to their views, limited in your perspectives and potentially closed to considering a different rationale.

Level 3: Changeable – Unfocused – Semi-open

The stereotype of a typical 'salesman' may help us describe your level of communication, in as much as you might appear a little pushy at times. You are likely to come across as changeable in your mood or personality when things are not going to plan. Although semi-open in your dialogue, you will not focus enough on them as a unique individual.

Level 4: Adaptable – Present – Open

You are a 'negotiator'. This means that you can adapt to changing situations when you need to while remaining focused on the current requirements of the other party. You demonstrate that you use open questioning to ease the communication along and are prepared to guide people towards an equitable outcome.

Level 5: Flexible – Engaging – Exploration

Your level of communication is that of a 'consultant'. Consultants are flexible in their approach to identifying the requirements of their stakeholders; they engage with their audience using powerful open questioning techniques and spend time exploring all the options and considerations.

Level 6: Versatile – Lucid – Unambiguous

Your level of the communication you use is that of a 'leader'. A 'leader', in terms of EI, is someone highly versatile in their interactions; they are incredibly lucid in their dialogue and completely unambiguous with their opinions and behaviours.

Developing your EI in this dimension

Style

We might well recall the last situation where there was that one person who sucked all the positive energy out of the meeting or the room like a vacuum cleaner. What we may not remember exactly is how they managed to do it!

Negative language is a critical resource of all 'energy sappers'. They use words that create disenchantment, foster disagreement, or promote arguments. And, for the majority of the time, they are not even aware of the impact they have.

The words we choose play a significant part in defining the environment we create and, thereby, the impact that we have on others.

A quick note on this point: if you have not already noticed, I have deliberately excluded all uses of the word 'but' throughout this book (except, of course, in the areas where we have been discussing positive and negative language), plus many more negative words and potentially disempowering negative phrases.

How do the words we choose to use daily actually measure up?

Activity

I would like for you to imagine that you are having a conversation with a friend and you are both deciding on where you would like to go on holiday next summer.

Part one

The only rule for this conversation is that each person starts each sentence with the words, *'Yes, but . . . '*
It might go something like this:

- First person: *'Yes, but* I would like to go to Spain.'
- Second person: *'Yes, but* Spain is too hot.'
- First person: *'Yes, but* there is so much to do in Spain.'
- Second person: *'Yes, but* it is full of tourists.'
- First person: *'Yes, but* that means we will meet lots of new people.'
- Second person: *'Yes, but* I don't like meeting new people.'

I am sure you will agree that the likelihood of this conversation resulting in a positive outcome is pretty low. It may have even resulted in negative feelings for both parties.

Yet, for many of us, we use those same words in much the same way in our everyday communications. In particular, we generally use the word *but* far too much!

The next time you are having a conversation with anyone, listen to the number of times they use the word but. It might just tell you a lot more about the current state of their EI than the other words they may be using!

As before, I would like for you to imagine that you are having a similar conversation with a friend and you are both deciding on where you would like to go on holiday next summer.

Activity

Part two

The only rule for this conversation is that one person starts each sentence with the words, '*Yes, and*' and the other with '*Yes, but*'.

It might go something like this:

- First person: '*Yes, and* I would like to go to Spain.'

- Second person: '*Yes, but* Spain is too hot.'

- First person: '*Yes, and* that means great suntans.'

- Second person: '*Yes, but* Spain is full of tourists.'

- First person: '*Yes, and* that means plenty of nightlife.'

- Second person: '*Yes, err*... well, I suppose that could be fun.'

Notice the difference?

It is not just some trick; it forms an integral part of human conditioning, going right back to the way that our mothers encouraged us often using subconscious *positive framing* techniques when we were very young.

Try it out yourself in a real discussion and what you will find is that, as soon as you start to use positive 'Yes, and' type words and phrases, people, irrespective of how negative they are, will begin to become more positive and warm to your ideas. You might even end up with both parties using a *Yes, and* approach and then being in total agreement. How lovely that would be!

Think also of the last time that you encountered a perfect salesperson, who effortlessly took you through the sales process and had you sign up for whatever it was they were selling. If we can pinpoint the language they used, what we will notice is that, even when they were empathising with us, they were using positive language to support the sales process.

Good salespeople need to be good communicators. They would not last long if their words were always negative. Yes, most good salespeople will have probably had to learn their trade through making mistakes, just like the rest of us.

From time to time, though, you will come across a natural-born salesperson (where positivity is in their nature), who exudes confidence, is always positive and usually smiles a lot. Maybe that is because they make so much money!

Listening

Consider a typical conversation where we are with a friend and where we are sitting in a noisy location; we may struggle to tune into all of what they are saying. We may miss the odd word or two, although, most of the time, we usually have enough context of the conversation to make sense of what they are saying.

We combine these conscious (cognitive) contextual clues with subconscious memories that help us to process each part of the information we hear.

The issues often come when we allow our erroneous thought processes to supersede those that are trying to make sense of the conversation.

We might have allowed our minds to wander off, only to eventually come back to the present moment when we may appear to have wholly misheard what they have been saying.

The act of really (actively) listening and hearing everything is hard work; we all have busy minds and trying to shut up and then shut out additional thoughts creates stress in our minds.

Tuning in requires us to focus our attention on the person and the subject matter of the conversation. We need to ensure that we are entirely in reception mode and not in transmit mode.

The simple answer to this is for us to adopt a position of *curiosity* and learning rather than just listening and nodding.

Ask questions. Yes, I know I keep saying that we must ask more questions, especially open questions that engage other people. Yet, those questions also miraculously enhance the curious nature of our cognitive minds when we ask them.

Even when the situation makes it inappropriate for us to ask questions verbally, at the very least, we should be seeking answers to those internal questions we form while the other person is speaking, while remaining alert and focused on them as an emotionally intelligent person should.

Activity

Practise active listening. To do this, I recommend that you find somewhere that is likely to be noisy, like sitting outside on a bench in a busy high street. As opposed to sitting on a bench in a quiet country park, which, although it might be good for the soul, may not help improve your listening skills.

- Focus on listening to only one sound at a time.
- Become curious about it and listen with intent.
- Note if there is any particular rhythm to the sound.
- Notice any variations in pitch or frequency.
- Concentrate on how this sound makes you feel, emotionally (happy, sad, annoyed, excited).
- Tune into the next sound, and repeat this exercise as much as you can, ideally honing it further for when you are next engaging with another person.

Practise this technique regularly to wake up your auditory skills and then fine-tune them to each conversation you have. Before too long, you will be amazed at the depth of new insights you will start to comprehend surrounding the people you are looking to engage in deeper conversation.

Often, when I am coaching someone, I focus just as much on the breath they take between the words. I hear the pauses they take, as well as the tone, level, pitch and frequency of the language they might use.

It gives rise to many more powerful insights around their situation and, quite often, it is those small, often missed parts of communication that help me in steering them towards finding a successful resolution.

Questioning

Questioning is the most naturally inbuilt resource that we have for finding our way across our lives. Yet, for some profound reason, it gets switched off pretty early in our development as human beings.

One of the biggest reasons for this is probably down to education. Imagine that, as a small child, after we first learn to speak, we also then learn how to question. I cannot count the number of times that I was almost driven to the edge of sanity by my three children continually asking, 'Why?' As I am sure that any parent will know, it is challenging, trying to ensure that they learn through providing adequate and useful answers.

Yet, I noticed that, as soon as each of my children started primary school, they stopped asking why and, in fact, they stopped asking many other types of questions.

I discussed this with my now-adult son, who is also now a parent himself, asking why this was. And he said that, early on, when he first went to school, he remembered a teacher responding to children when they asked, 'Why?' mainly, with the same answer: 'Because it is!' rather than providing the children with explanations, which might have derailed their particular lesson plan!

Whatever the reason, even with today's far more informed teaching techniques, we all stop asking useful questions early on in our lives. Maybe, this is because we don't want to sound or appear stupid to other people; or possibly, because it related to our earlier lives when we were discouraged because it was regarded as disrespectful to ask too many questions.

Whatever the reason, we need to question and use appropriate questioning techniques to enable us to continue to grow and develop as adults, irrespective of our age.

We are going to look again at the *Logical Levels* model that we used earlier in Chapter 10 to help us with this section.

Through asking a person 'open questions' and linking those answers into more 'open questions' or, at the very least, providing the appropriate sounds or movements like nodding or smiling, will encourage them to share more.

Ask who, what, when, where and how questions at each level to gain information at that level. Ask *why* and it will take us up to the next level and, therefore, deepen our level of understanding.

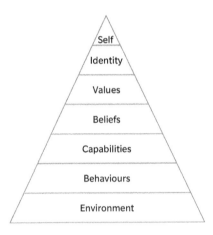

When we start to ask open questions at an *environmental* level, they will appear less intrusive, more general and, therefore, more natural to answer.

An example might be, 'How long have you been working here?' Friendly and relaxed, straightforward, and always a good opener for a conversation!

We then might broaden this conversation by asking more open questions: who, what, when, where or how, ideally, directly linked to their answers, and begin to understand more about their role, the company, the department, or whatever else we wanted to gain at an 'environmental' level.

However, if we wanted to discover more about the person and less about the environment or situation, we might just find this type of questioning unhelpful and may need to ask *why*?

'Five whys (or 5 whys) is an iterative interrogative technique used to explore the cause-and-effect relationships underlying a particular problem. The primary goal of the method is to determine the root cause of a defect or problem by repeating the question 'Why?'. Each answer forms the basis of the next question.'

The trouble with using 'Five whys' is that taking the conversation up one level at a time by just asking 'why' can feel intimidating for both parties.

A possible way of doing this reasonably comfortably is to ask why at an appropriate time and in conjunction with the answers they have just given us. An example might be, 'Oh, that is interesting that you have been working here for such a long time; why is that?'

Provided the question is a *why* question, it will always take the conversation up to the next level, in this case, the behaviour level. An alternative to the *'why'* question is often needed, especially if we are involved in any coaching conversations.

By linking one of the other open question words directly with the term *'specifically'*, it serves just as well as a why question. It will take the conversation up to the next level, without any uncomfortable feelings of interrogation.

Example: 'What, specifically, has kept you working here for so long?'

It is easy enough to move down the model too, by asking an open question directly related to one of the levels below the one in which we are currently working.

For example: if we were working at the *capability* level, I might ask, 'What *behaviours* might be useful?' Or, to go down to the *environment* level, I might ask, 'What changes might we see in the office?' Or 'Where might this make a difference?'

Note: this is a powerful technique. We need to be forever mindful when taking the conversation above the *values* level and working at the *identity* level. We should not do so unless the participant has expressly given us their permission.

Important: we should never go above the *identity* level to *self* and, thereby, arbitrarily stray into the field of psychology unless, of course, we are fully qualified to do so.

Through plenty of practice using this technique, we become proficient in ensuring that we can understand others enough and remove all assumptions to build healthy dialogue, maybe even resulting in a broader range of solutions to problems or issues.

Often, just noting where a barrier may exist, at which level, will enable us to pinpoint accurately what actions we should take with the other person to help remedy or enhance a situation.

Activity

Make it about them – once you have identified a willing person to help you practise this technique, start by asking them open questions only at the environment level.

When you hear something that intrigues you, ask them a linked *why* (or secret why) question to take you up to the behavioural level.

Repeat this process, without just asking *why* to each answer they give, expanding your knowledge of them through other open questions, until you have identified at least *one* of their core values.

chapter 12

Team dynamics

What is it?

In terms of emotional intelligence, the 'team' dimension represents our ability to build, support, influence, resolve conflict and work together with others to achieve common goals.

Efficient team members will possess complementary skills that generate results through delivering coordinated effort, allowing each member to utilise their fundamental skills and abilities.

The team dimension covers:

- Team builder
- Influencing
- Conflict resolution

Your dimension feedback

Use the *average* score that you recorded for this particular PEIP dimension to review the relevant feedback, as detailed by the corresponding levels of 1 to 6 below.

Level 1: Non-manager – Non-influencer – Passive

Your highly independent mindset will not always hold you in a strong position with other people, it will lead to a lack of respect from them and potentially reduce opportunities for your personal and professional development. Independent people do not make great people managers; nor do they make great influencers as their passive nature is more likely to inhibit rather than encourage high engagement.

Level 2: Support – Ineffectual – Resolution

The level of confidence that you have in dealing with some of the more challenging people to reach a joint resolution is low. Although you may believe that you support the team, your level of ability in dealing with some members is likely to be ineffectual.

Level 3: Remote – Persuader – Acceptance

You appear to be isolated from other people; this might well be because you work or live alone. Although you demonstrate a reasonable ability to persuade others, you are likely to accept and adapt to their views or position due to not being confident enough to challenge them, even when you know you may well be right.

Level 4: Harmony – Balance – Challenge

You are a good team player. You help balance the attributes of everyone against the requirements for the task in hand. You feel comfortable in dealing with challenges across the majority of situations and people.

Level 5: Enhancing – Alignment – Enablement

You are the team's coach; you seek to enhance the capabilities of each of the team members, through helping them to align their strengths and abilities against tasks that, ultimately, enable the entire team to flourish.

Level 6: Synergistic – Compelling – Mediator

You are the team captain; whether that is deliberately through a title or the role you take, you elegantly combine the capabilities of each team member to create a synergistic and mutually beneficial environment for people to excel. You compel others to engage with and support their colleagues and effectively mediate a joined-up resolution when any minor conflicts surface.

Developing your EI in this dimension

Team builder

Being a competent team builder is an integral part of most management roles. It is also an essential capability to have when trying to organise groups of people outside of a typical working context.

Importantly, for teams to become productive, each of the team members must be fully aligned with the same sense of vision or purpose, and then effectively motivated to make that purpose a reality.

Building a team requires more than just an idea of the direction of travel on which the team needs to embark. Each team member needs the knowledge of the destination itself, and then only through *their* regular contribution of ideas or suggestions might the entire group feel empowered to define the nature of the journey towards that goal.

Very often, repeated team building mistakes occur when the team builder or manager decides on the destination (*what*) as well as the mode of travel towards it (*how*) themselves, without consultation with other members of the group. This command-and-control functionality is most likely to disenfranchise most team members.

Although they may turn up for the work, their hearts and minds will not be in it and, more often than not, the project itself will be in jeopardy and might even fail.

For many, the nature of the goal itself, *what* needs to happen, might be predetermined by role, type of business or the work we undertake. In these cases, each person in the team must be allowed to contribute to defining *how* we are going to make it happen.

Since the beginning of the global COVID-19 pandemic outbreak, remote working has become a way of life. Working remotely from the office or business is likely to delay team building to some extent, and we need to become ever more mindful of the unique requirements of each of our team members.

Online team meetings and group chats are a great way of ensuring that members feel they are contributing. However, we also need to be more vigilant in supporting those quieter souls who find online interaction difficult or confusing.

Personal, one-to-one chats are still crucial for everyone, irrespective of being in an office, remote working or home-based. Everyone needs time to review, discuss and talk through the work that they do, and we all need coaching to help us develop those skills and capability that might be holding us back from contributing more.

An issue that often perplexes me around team building is when I see or hear a manager who has a preference towards one or more individuals in their team. Through sharing similar personality or character traits, they may often choose them over others to complete particular tasks, irrespective of their skill or capability.

The only emotionally intelligent reason why one person should be chosen over another to complete a task is because they either can do the job or they are in the process of learning how to do the job.

Building a team requires fairness and consistency. If we allow our preferences to intervene in ensuring this, we will not be enabling the organisation of people to function effectively as a whole – remember that diversity and inclusion are paramount.

Of course, there are situations as a team leader in which we have to make a judgement call and, sometimes, that call will upset other members of the group. Yet, provided that we are always fair and consistent across each of our interactions, these situations will be less.

In essence, building a team requires us to ensure that we are true to our values and are demonstrating our justified beliefs through the interaction we have with every team member.

When team building is not working, it creates a raft of different emotions from each of the team members. Some of these may be verbal, although I would add that, in many cases, they are likely also to be physically displayed.

As a team builder, it is essential to identify when people are unhappy, stressed, demotivated, unsure, insecure or angry. Some of these emotions might be easy enough to spot, although others require us to become ever more vigilant of the subtle changing emotional natures of the people involved.

We need to continuously *watch*, *listen* and *learn* through each team interaction and pick up on any of the signs of team imbalance. Providing immediate group or individual feedback is then essential to developing team members as well as restoring the team's balance.

Activity

Consider a time when you have been a member of a team, and either did not feel as though you entirely fitted into the group, or you felt that others were not as supported as you may have been.

▶

1 What elements were missing in how supported you/they were by the team itself or the team leader?

2 How does this make you feel, specifically?

3 What could have changed in that situation?

4 How might you ensure that you do not allow this to happen to someone else?

5 What are you going to commit to doing, differently, when building a team?

Influencing

Delegates often ask me to help them with improving a particularly tricky relationship they have with another person or persons. My immediate answer is pretty much always the same, and that is, they will have to adjust the relationship that they have with themselves first!

Years of experience in the field of behavioural science have taught me that there is a crucial principle to making relationships work, and that is *'you have to be prepared to go there first'*.

If we want to change the behaviours, reactions, responses of another, we must change those things in ourselves that might be driving those responses.

Consider our emotional state when we encounter a problematic relationship:

- How threatened, overwhelmed, superior/inferior or negative are we being towards them?

- How comfortable are we at making direct eye contact with them?

- What is happening to us on a physical level? (Breathing, posture, voice – tone, control, even pitch.)

- How confident are we feeling inside ourselves?

- What other, more subtle emotional signals might we already be sending out before we open our mouth to speak?

We are all guilty of allowing different external influences to shape our responses. These can be as simple as how the person looks or sounds, to more complex experiences of being let down, a lack of trust or non-conformity.

Whatever influence may have contributed to our current state of thinking about that other person, we might want to consider the impact of allowing that influence to pervade the relationship going forward.

Once we have managed to clear any of the debris that might have accumulated within our mind about this other person, it is then essential for us first to approach them with neutrality.

In other words, start afresh by having a good relationship with them. Consider initially making the next contact we have with them about them and not about us or, for that matter, any other subject.

Once we start to make our focus *about* the other person, it changes the emotional dynamic.

Activity

Think about a person with whom you would like to have a better relationship.

Write down all the things that you factually know about them; like their personal preferences, their wants and needs, how they might currently perceive you. What makes them happy or sad? What are they struggling with at home or work?

If you have just created a huge list, then you are likely to be in serious trouble with this relationship, sorry to be the bearer of unfortunate tidings and all that.

Using an emotionally intelligent approach, you will need to consider all the evidence of how you managed to influence the negative situation that you have inadvertently or deliberately created!

You might then need to arrange a convenient time for the pair of you to have a very honest and frank discussion, where you both agree that the situation needs to change.

Before you get started, you will also need to agree that there is to be no blame on either side.

Then, you will have to initiate the discussion where you accept responsibility for every little thing that may have transpired in the relationship, irrespective of whether or not the fault was yours.

An example might be: 'I am sorry. It's my fault that we don't seem to be getting along at the moment, I have been . . .'

Our acceptance of the issues relating to any problem sends out a very different set of emotional and physical signals to the other person. Their reaction, although possibly still a little tense, might well surprise us.

We all have the same emotional needs, and one of the strongest is acceptance by other people. When we take responsibility for the problem/s in the relationship, we are appealing to those fundamental instincts and, more often than not, the issues will get resolved.

If, on the other hand, our list is very light, there is a high chance that the most significant part of the problem here is that we simply have not made the right connection with this person. The resulting action we need to take will be to ensure that we make it our business to get to know them better.

You may be amazed that, once you do get to know this person, they are entirely different from what you had imagined. We could find that they have a lot in common with us, even the same inadequacies, fears or concerns.

We are influenced, rightly or wrongly, by other people. We become deliberately or inadvertently drawn to their perspectives, attitudes and beliefs and, the stronger those beliefs become, the more significant the effect on us.

Observe any typical situation between an influential boss and a subordinate, where the boss is very confident, highly knowledgeable and extremely well-connected, and we see the effect the influence has on the subordinate.

A good boss will be inspiring and motivating, encouraging the subordinate's perspectives and steering them towards developing their knowledge and capability in a variety of different ways.

A bad boss will intimidate the subordinate with their knowledge; they will not encourage or motivate the employee, and the results will generally speak for themselves, where the subordinate is likely to become fearful and reserved and less likely to develop their potential as a result.

Activity

Now consider the influence you have at home and work, and ask yourself these questions:

- How do I currently influence the different people in my life?
- What might they say about how much I influence them?
- How might I influence them better?
- What do I need to start doing?
- What do I need to stop doing?
- When am I going to make this happen?

Conflict resolution

During times of conflict, each of our two amygdala sends a series of chemical messages or neurotransmissions, usually of adrenalin and cortisol, to flood our nervous systems to get us ready for the fight or flight responses we discussed in Chapter 4.

For those of us who choose *fight*, our muscle groups are in both attack and defence mode, primed and ready for the physical exertions of a battle.

When we choose *flight* as the often more healthy option in the battle scenario, a different muscle group is involved with moving us out of danger.

Now, let us consider the impact of the particular muscle groups associated with *fight* and *flight*, especially those responsible for the movement of the face and eyes, and then think about how these will change our facial expression in each case.

If we choose the wrong emotional response in a given situation, we might very well be sending out entirely false signals to the other people involved!

It is worth thinking about, especially if, due to the nature of our role, we find ourselves in situations of conflict on a day-to-day basis.

Conflict is good. It helps us determine where issues or problems exist and then, if appropriately managed, often it will result in a positive outcome for all parties involved.

So, what gets in the way of conflict being positive?

The simple answer is that *we* do. We allow our internal dialogue to inform our emotional responses, which quite often lead to the wrong chemical release, which then leads to interpretation, rightly or wrongly, of our actual intentions by the other party.

Dealing with conflict is quite straightforward if we are emotionally intelligent about it. The more we *remove* our emotions from the situation, concentrate on what is genuine and not supposed, the clearer the facts become. That, in turn, will help steer us towards a resolution.

Let's imagine a scenario where we need to have a conversation with a person with whom we have a conflict over a particularly sticky issue.

We could quickly end up addressing the situation purely from our perspective and not theirs, which might result in creating even more conflict.

The emotionally intelligent approach is to use an *enquiry*-based system to determine the situation from *their* perspective and, if required, to then coach them effortlessly towards a mutually agreeable solution.

Example

1   Ask them to help you solve *the* problem.
    'Hi, John. I need you to help as we appear to have a problem with XYZ.'

2   Be upfront, transparent and unemotional about briefly
    detailing the problem and *not* the *behaviours* associated
    with it.
    'Last week X and Y were late.'

3   Only provide *factual* evidence that supports the problem
    and *not* any of your/other *emotions* associated with it.
    'This resulted in Z being mis-reported in our figures to head office.'

4   Ask them if these are the *only* issues *we* need to resolve.
    *'What other issues do you think we might need to resolve at
    this time?'*

5   Let them talk without interruption (just maybe nod and
    encourage).

6   Ask them how *we* might resolve these (and any other)
    issues *we* have identified.
    'How might we resolve these effectively?'

7   *Let them finish* talking. Do not interrupt and do not ask any
    more questions until they have finished.

8   Thank them for their input and then ask what *they* need to
    do differently moving forward.
    *'Thanks, John, that was most helpful. What might you do to
    help move this forward?'*

9   Ask them how we might measure and track any progress
    towards the new objective.
    'That is great. How might we track any progress with this?'

10 Commit to working with them to achieve this.
    *'Excellent. Let's keep the dialogue flowing and ensure that we
    keep each other updated as we progress.'*

There are, of course, many other techniques for dealing with conflict
and the difficult conversations that surround it. I can highly recommend Susan Scott's book *Fierce Conversations: Achieving success at
work and in life, one conversation at a time.*

Activity

Think of an existing or recent conflict situation where you were involved, either directly or indirectly.

- How much emotional energy did you, personally, use up?
- Was this the most effective use of your capability?
- How might you gain longer-term results in the future?
- What needs to happen differently?
- How and when will you make these changes?

chapter 13

Leadership capability

What is it?

In this dimension, leadership relates to the use of our sensory perception, or intuition, to guide our words and actions. It further describes how we inspire others to follow a pathway, and it defines how we adapt to the changing landscape of requirements along the route.

The leadership dimension covers:

- Intuition
- Inspiration
- Adaptability

Your dimension feedback

Use the *average* score that you recorded for this particular PEIP dimension to review the relevant feedback, as detailed by the corresponding levels of 1 to 6 below.

Level 1: Challenged – Uninspiring – Fixed

You demonstrate a somewhat insular leadership style because you find it difficult to read and understand people, you lack inspiration for yourself, let alone others, and you remain fixed in your opinions and perspectives.

Level 2: Unclear – Selective – Indistinct

Siloed leadership best describes this level. You are often unclear about what other people may require of you; you are selective with whom you engage, and you are indistinct concerning the direction of travel to ensure overall success.

Level 3: Instinctive – Comfortable – Adaptable

Your leadership style is open. You use instinct to guide some of your words and actions. You create a comfortable place for people to live and work, and you adapt to changing situations when you need to. Yet, you are not inspiring the people you lead, which may result in complacency and unfulfilled goals.

Level 4: Adjusts – Encourages – Flexible

You are flexible in your leadership style. You adjust to the changing dynamics of the situation and use the right level of encouragement in bringing people along with you. Be careful not to become overly flexible as this will result in uncertainty of purpose and the actions required.

Level 5: Astute – Attuned – Accommodating

You are an intuitive leader. You are very astute when picking up on the actual requirements of the people you lead, you comfortably attune to their needs and accommodate them whenever and wherever possible. Yet, there is a small possibility that you might become so engrossed in the people element that you could lose sight of the bigger picture or goal.

Level 6: Intuitive – Inspirational – Engaging

You are an inspirational leader! You demonstrate that you are very intuitive, adaptable, astute and highly engaging. Be mindful that people will also be looking to follow your example and, thereby, lead them towards overall success.

Developing your EI in this dimension

Intuition

People often think that our sixth sense, being intuition, is some mysterious and otherworldly capability of individuals who report having an ability to know things before other people or before they happen – where the sixth sense also works in isolation of the other five senses, namely: sight, sound, smell, taste and touch.

I reason that this is not the case. We all have a sixth sense that most of us use daily, and it is what informs the *preferences* we have about things, people or situations, as well as letting us know when we might be in danger (the hair-raising-on-the-back-of-our-neck stuff).

In neuro-linguistic programming (NLP), practitioners use the word *kinaesthetic* to describe an emotional state or a physical feeling like hot or cold, hard or soft. In Science, the definition of *kinaesthetic* relates to a person's awareness of the position and movement of their body, using sensory organs (proprioceptors), which are found in muscles and joints.

Irrespective of our preference between using *kinaesthetics* and/ or *feelings* to describe individual aspects within emotional states, we can agree that we are mainly alluding to the same thing.

I further reason that, when we choose to combine all of our physical and emotional senses, we are using our sixth sense. We might feel a lot more comfortable referring to our sixth sense as *intuition*, as this may also be far easier for others to comprehend.

Tuning into our intuition is a lot easier than we might, at first, think. It is working for us, all of the time, even while you are reading this. Your senses are picking up all the sounds, smells, changes in temperature, physical (like, touch, hunger or pain) and emotional feelings that you may be having at this very moment.

Our brain is working hard to keep us safe and well. It is scanning our environment constantly to inform us of those minute changes that may affect our equilibrium. Whether we choose to act on those inputs is down to personal choice and preference.

Our intuition becomes heightened when we are in a state of flow. The subconscious part of our mind records every sight, sound, feeling and sensation. When we are in a state of flow, we have direct access to all conscious, as well as subconscious, neurology.

Just like tuning a television to find the most reliable transmission, we need to tune into all of our senses to enable us to become far more intuitive:

- *Listening:* turning up our internal volume on what we hear in conversations, by understanding where the emphasis is, the use of certain words, and being completely aware of any inclinations used. By just listening to understand, without judgement or internal dialogue, we gain profound insight and, therefore, deeper resonance with the speaker.

- *Seeing:* looking at every single detail present in the situation, such as eye movements, posture, gestures and other small involuntary movements, will help us gain an advantage by understanding any real and perceived problems.

- *Feeling:* turning up the dial on our feelings and trusting them will bring us a mass of new capability. They will inform our decisions; they will help us provide solutions, which may, potentially, save us a considerable amount of time.

Allowing our intuition to be more present in our life enables us to become more present in every situation. It helps to raise our game to the next level. Intuition provides us with so much more than we currently could imagine or possibly believe.

One last point. Intuition is already hard-wired into our whole person, our very being, it is free, and it would be a real shame if we denied its existence and did not use it effectively.

Activity

- Close your eyes for a minute or two and concentrate on the different sounds, smells and tastes that are around you.

- Then, focus your attention on what you can physically feel, like hot or cold, soft or hard things, like the surface where you are sitting or standing.

- Finally, tune into your emotional feelings and relate these directly back to all the other senses you have just experienced.

Inspiration

Inspiration is a mental process that engages us to do or feel something different. It can be attributed to creativity, although this does not always have to be the case.

Our inspiration comes from a combination of the various sensory inputs that our brain receives. The feelings we gain as a result of these stimuli release chemicals through the different opiate-type receptors in our brain that give us a mental high and make us feel fantastic.

Of course, we are not all the same, and that means that different stimuli affect different people in different ways. Some people will be more affected by a beautiful sunset (visual) than the sheer wonder of an orchestral performance of Mozart (auditory), for example.

As I am sitting here in my office writing these words, I am looking (*visual*) over to my pond and watching the dragonflies hover, and how the butterflies are flitting between the different fauna in the surrounding area.

That, for me, is inspiring! I am sitting here typing with a massive smile on my face and feeling great (*kinaesthetic*). I am finding that the words are flowing a little more comfortably in my head (*auditory*) than they were earlier this morning when I first started writing and, who knows, this new flow state might even help with my words to inspire you?

OK, back to reality. What inspires me will not necessarily encourage you. We are different. If we want to inspire individuals, then we have to tailor the experience we craft towards their individual preferences, and that can be tricky, especially if we are working with large groups of people.

The secret is to find something that is going to be inspirational for everyone, and that means changing the lens a little on our perspective of what is and is not inspirational.

A way of starting the process is to think about our audience as a single entity and, starting from what we already know about them, we can begin to manage our perceptions by first checking that we are not making any unqualified assumptions.

Next, we need to determine that our mode of communication will excite them, not just ourselves. Because we know that auditory people prefer to listen, visual people like to see, and kinaesthetic people prefer to emotionally and physically feel, we might need to consider an approach that will enable all three of these.

An excellent example of this is to think of a good advertisement on a commercial radio station. While the medium itself is pretty fixed as *auditory*, through the creative use of sound effects and dialogue, listeners are engaged using their imagination (*visual*) to make an emotional (*feeling*-based) connection with the product.

The same techniques happen in television commercials, although it is a little more straightforward as two of the three senses are already engaged, being sight and sound. This only then leaves the advertiser to help us make an emotional connection with the product and, if we do, we get hooked.

The second part of developing inspiration is to identify our audience's key motivation. In other words, why they have shown up, in whatever way, to engage with us or our subject matter.

Take a business leader who is looking to inspire his team through a difficult time of change. If he concentrated only on the value of the bottom-line profits for his shareholders, his staff would not feel particularly inspired to do more.

If, however, the leader concentrated on the impact of an increase in bottom-line profits on employees' paycheques, his staff would certainly be inspired to do more.

It is the simple realignment of what is most likely to motivate an audience that makes the difference in how inspired they will become as a result of it.

Unfortunately, we have all been on the receiving end of some pretty uninspiring communication, which has only served to disengage our emotional intelligence and not make full use of it.

Activity

Think about who has inspired you recently. It could have been at work or at home. You may have been inspired by something as simple as watching a young person go out of their way to help a blind person across a busy road. Or, it might be a recent broadcast where someone was trying to make a difference to the whole of humanity.

1 How did this motivate you into taking action, changing behaviour or achieving a goal?

2 How did they make you feel at the time?

3 What could they have done to inspire you even further?

4 What do you need to start doing differently from today so that you become an inspiration to others?

Adaptability

Adapting our capability to rapidly and efficiently learn new skills, or being able to change our behaviours in response to the evolving requirements of a situation, is one of the most sought-after capabilities in leadership. Yet, unfortunately, very often it is overlooked in the hiring process!

Highly adaptable leaders are flexible in their approach to solving complex problems, and they can efficiently react to rapid environmental and local situational changes. They work well on their own as well as use their flexibility to manage multiple teams and workstreams.

What is there not to like?

While we may all agree that adaptability is an essential aspect of leadership, many of us find the internal mental process of adapting immensely challenging at times.

We get stuck in our ways; we like things the way that they are, we follow rituals or routines because they are comfortable and because we don't want to unsettle the internal balance we have established in our minds.

Accepting that change is a constant process, which is going on in every aspect within our bodies, our minds and across our entire world, is probably going to be the best place for us to start.

However, what that *acceptance* means, for some, is the fundamental realisation that life is transitory, where there will never be a permanent state of anything.

My Dad (God bless him) used to say, 'Grass grows!' whenever I was struggling to accept a situation and adapt to it. In other words, to stop wasting time procrastinating, get on and do something about it and do not let the grass grow under your feet by standing still.

I love the analogy of grass. We can cut it down; we might even burn it back or pull it out by its roots; it will still grow back, given the right environmental conditions and time. That is the adaptive nature of grass.

It is also the nature of human beings. We survive as a species and have done for thousands of years. We flourish and grow, maybe not all at once or in the same location, yet, we will continue to survive because we can adapt.

Sometimes, adapting to something takes a lot of EI, especially if we can't find any logical reason for the change to happen. We may, then, try to determine the facts by analysing what data we have available to us and, if it still does not all make sense to us personally, we dig in our heels and then refuse to adapt.

It is in times like this when we can use our EI most to help guide our thinking away from just the facts, as we may have chosen to understand them currently, and consider other people's perspectives. Recognising and acknowledging their emotions, their reasons or their implicit thinking might help us to adapt our own.

Activity

Consider how adaptable you are currently and what you might need to focus on to help improve this further.

If you tend to follow routines or rituals, try adapting one of these, for example, like finding a different route to drive to and from work each day.

This approach will help remove some of the tension created by following too rigid a routine, and you may well uncover new rewards through different experiences and discoveries.

chapter 14

Approach to change

What is it?

In the *change catalyst* dimension, we are looking at those multiple strengths that promote and support the change in guiding an organisation of people towards the ultimate delivery of the outcomes they collectively require.

The change catalyst dimension covers:

- Instigator
- Supporter
- Agent

Your dimension feedback

Use the *average* score that you recorded for this particular PEIP dimension to review the relevant feedback, as detailed by the corresponding levels of 1 to 6 below.

Level 1: Appeaser – Unsupportive – Challenger

You appear to be past-focused, where you prefer the way you used to do things as opposed to how you do them now or in the future. You are likely to resist change through becoming unsupportive and cynical about it, challenging the process, the people involved, and their reasons for wanting to bring about any change.

Level 2: Opportunist – Helper – Agreement

You appear to be present-focused concerning change; this means that you might only support change if there is an immediate benefit for yourself, in which case you are likely to help the change process by gaining the agreement of the parties involved.

Level 3: Resourceful – Worker – Activist

You are resourceful when it comes to the change process; you readily seek to find better ways of doing things and are prepared to put in the extra hours required to ensure that the change happens in the right way at the right time. You may want to consider becoming less of an activist and more of an enabler of change, as some people will not be entirely comfortable with a potentially 'gung-ho' approach.

Level 4: Adaptor – Supporter – Enabler

You support people through the change process, adapting, if necessary, to the process elements required along the way to suit their needs, while still enabling the process itself to evolve. You may need to consider taking a more structured and less free-flow approach if you are required to oversee the actual change process itself.

Level 5: Challenger – Encourager – Improver

You are future-focused, you like to challenge the status quo, encouraging people to adopt and adapt to a wide range of ideas, systems, processes and even behaviours. You continuously seek to improve every element of your world, the only caveat being that you may, sometimes, forget to identify all the impacts of the change on others.

Level 6: Ambassador – Planned – Progressive

You are the agent of change! Your detailed, planned approach to engaging all the stakeholders involved in any change situation ensures that you make assured and measured progress. Your skill at being the ambassador of the change itself enables others to accept, adapt and settle into new routines quickly and effortlessly.

Developing your EI in this dimension

Instigator

According to Deloitte: 'change instigators' have an unambiguous view of their destination. They are experts at painting a picture of this destination and motivating others to follow and execute it.

Ironically, change is likely to be the most consistent thing going on in today's world. Gone are the days of everything being comfortable and straightforward.

We have to adapt daily to new technologies, new processes and ever more information and, of course, new ways of creating the right balance in our personal lives to keep up with all the changes that are going on around us.

Although many people might say that we are creatures of habit and that change is always going to be difficult, we are, in fact, animals of change, as we have been adapting and changing as a human species for hundreds and thousands of years.

So, why would change become uncomfortable for some and not for others?

The answer lies in the particular version or type of world that we have created for ourselves. If we are too *past*-focused, preferring the old ways to the new and dislike moving away from established routines, it is highly likely that any change will become a threat to our emotional equilibrium.

Whereas, if we accept that change is an integral part of life and are enthusiastic about the *future* and look to find the *potential* in all things, our emotional equilibrium becomes used to an ever-changing landscape and, therefore, adjusts accordingly.

Change instigators seek to find inspiration from both inside and outside of an organisational context. Their primary aim is to identify different and improved methods of performing functional and non-functional tasks.

For many, instigating change is not the highest thing on our to-do list; mainly because we prefer to follow the comfortable routines we have fallen into across our work and home life.

We often resist change because the imbalance to our internal, emotional equilibrium might then lead us to experience confusion, uncertainty and, potentially, insecurity through allowing a change to happen, irrespective of any potential long-term rewards that the change may bring.

We also need to understand that upsetting the status quo is likely to create some level of resistance, particularly from those most affected in the change process. This resistance might even become hostility, if it is not managed early enough in the process.

Being a change instigator requires us to think clearly about the impact of change on people, and that means often thinking outside of our levels of emotional comfort. We need to challenge both our own and other people's thinking in the right way.

Therefore, instigating change is not just about coming up with better ways of doing things; it requires a deep understanding of how those changes will, ultimately, affect the people and the processes involved.

Finding a comfortable structure to enable the acceptance of any change process should be the first item on our agenda and, to this end, I have outlined below the type of things that we might need to include on our to-do list:

1 *Understand and detail the impact* that the change will have on the organisation and all the people involved.

2 *Build an emotional business case* outlining all of the features and advantages of the change from a people perspective.

3 *Build a technical business case* outlining which internal process and mechanisms will be improved or enhanced.

4 *Build a financial business case* outlining the financial benefits and implications of the change for the business.

5 *Engage the informal organisation* in the change process.
   We are usually comfortable engaging our formal line management and stakeholders. There will always be other *informal* stakeholders who will hear about the project and then, maybe, try and deflect its course.

6 *Set the example* of modelling any change yourself.

7 *Monitor, evaluate and manage* the change process and the people involved.

Activity

Use this list as a foundation to bring about a real-life change in your life, your work or your home. It could be something relatively personal like the revamp of a room in your home or changing your car. Or, maybe, it could have far broader implications affecting more people, such as the revamp of an entire office, business, management team, product line or, even, an organisational process.

Supporter

Change supporters are those people who accept that the change is essential, and it also describes those who will be critical in helping us to bring the change to fruition.

Having already identified the individual elements that go towards bringing that change about effectively, we now need to consider the support required at each stage for both our formal and informal stakeholders.

Before we begin this process, we need to identify which of these stakeholders is most likely to be *past*-focused and, thereby, a potential derailer in the change process.

At the same time, we need to identify those stakeholders expected to be *future*-focused and, thereby, a supporter or even an enabler of the proposed change.

A simple method of doing this would be to carry out a quick survey where, based on a standard multiple-choice framework, we can identify where our stakeholders' preferences lie.

There are many online tools available to support this process, like SurveyMonkey, SmartSurvey or Typeform, where we can easily create a multiple-choice questionnaire to send via email to all of our stakeholders.

Alternatively, using an internal email, intranet, or even a familiar face-to-face type questionnaire, is likely to get the same results.

Choosing the right methodology to engage with each of the stakeholders and then provide them with the proper support will be entirely based on our unique requirements of that change situation. Although the objectives will still remain the same:

1 Name the change.

2 Explain the reasons for the change.

3 Identify who and what will be affected by the change.

4 Detail how the change process will work.

5 Explain what support is available for each stakeholder.

6 Explain how they can access support.

7 Provide time scales.

8 Identify potential impacts on business as usual.

9 Provide essential contact/s information.

Irrespective of the change itself, the key to ensuring that everything runs smoothly is to be open in our communication, keeping everyone informed and updated on any progress and providing regular support for those who may be struggling.

Activity

Using the information you collected in the last activity, identify how you might support this change process going forward.

- What needs to happen to make the process comfortable for everyone?
- How will you support the people involved?
- What do you need to do differently for all future changes?
- Why will you stick to this new approach?
- What will happen if you do not?
- What change/s will you commit to for yourself?

Agent

The individual or group of people who undertake the task of initiating and managing change in an organisation is known as a change agent. A change agent, through their preference of outward curiosity, identifies the potential solution or opportunity, as well as how to incorporate them effectively into existing frameworks.

One of the biggest challenges in organisations of any type is recognising potential growth opportunities and then bringing those opportunities to fruition through demonstrating flexibility and resilience across their existing and potential markets.

As change agents, we need to adopt the curious mindset required to identify these potential opportunities in the first place, and then adjust our EI to reflect the same level of flexibility and resilience in determining the benefits to the organisation and the people involved.

The same level of EI will be required to ensure that our focus remains equally balanced between bottom-line profit and the necessary human endeavour needed to meet it.

Change agents are never happy with here and now, they are always curious about how things work and, indeed, how they might be improved or done entirely differently.

Curiosity is a component link between the cognitive and the EI part of the brain. It primes the mind ready for learning new things.

When we become curious, we are using a lot more than just a single neural pathway. We are using all our stored subconscious data to make sense of the situation.

We then rationalise that data using our emotional perspective, which may be influenced by our visual, auditory, and even our kin-aesthetic signal processing.

At the same time, our cognitive mind is trying to make sense of the situation and then come up with alternative solutions.

Curiosity is a shared process across almost all living entities on our planet. Curiosity keeps us safe and it also evolves and develops our species. The more curious we become, the faster we can adapt, grow and develop.

What stops people becoming curious?

The answer is just routine, ritualistic or habitual behaviour, which quite often is underscored by complacency.

If we want to keep growing as individuals, we must break any or all of these rigid behaviours that stop us developing a new mindset based on possibility and the potential in all things.

Activity

1 Identify which habits are most likely to be stopping you from becoming more curious and then answer the following questions for each one:

   • How does this (negative) habit inhibit you?

- What alternative (positive) habit could you replace this with?

- How will you know when you have changed this habit?

2 Focus your curiosity on a single thing; it might be something singular like a blade of grass, or something bigger like a tree, the shape of a building, or the ripples on the water surrounding a fountain (anything that you can focus on).

- What are the intricate details you can pick out?

- How do these elements relate to one another, specifically?

- How could you change the relationship between these elements?

- What is the outcome of those combined changes?

chapter 15

Collaborating with others

What is it?

The collaboration dimension is about when more than one person or equalitarian group works collectively to fulfil a unified task or complete a joint objective.

The collaboration dimension covers:

- Networking
- Groupworking
- Long-term relationships

Your dimension feedback

Use the *average* score that you recorded for this particular PEIP dimension to review the relevant feedback, as detailed by the corresponding levels of 1 to 6 below.

Level 1: Isolated – Solo – Insular

You appear detached from other people; this may be because you choose to have a solo role or the role itself determines this. The issues potentially relating to this are those of isolation and potential exclusion by others, as the perception of you might be that of being insular and guarded.

Level 2: Self-focused – Remote – Insecure

You may appear to others as being a little self-focused or too remote at times; this might well be down to you having a lack of confidence in yourself or because you demonstrate elements of insecurity through your evident behaviours or attitude.

Level 3: Social – Functional – Average

You appear to collaborate with other people merely to appease the functional aspects of your activities or role. Although your social skills might seem to be pretty average, it might indicate that there is a lack of self-belief when you are collaborating with others, especially if you view their capabilities to be significantly stronger than your own.

Level 4: External – Sharer – Team mate

You are an excellent team player; you confidently share information with others as part of your professional and private life. People will readily rely on you for help and always know where to come when they might need a sounding board to vent their frustrations.

Level 5: Marketer – Supporter – Communicator

You use strong communication skills to market and promote collaboration both professionally and personally. You leverage your networks to help develop your capabilities and knowledge; in return, you comfortably support those people you collaborate with when there is a need.

Level 6: Networker – Collaborator – Facilitator

You use the knowledge and capabilities of people in your extensive business-specific, professional and private networks exceptionally well. You provide each person with whom you collaborate with genuine support, guidance or advice as necessarily required from yourself, as well as enabling them to engage with other people from your network with highly relevant expertise.

Developing your EI in this dimension

Emotionally intelligent people are natural collaborators because they competently understand that, as human beings, we do not function particularly well in isolation.

Collaboration is where it is at if we want to get ahead in this world. We all need to collaborate with the people who can support our journey through our extraordinary lives, providing us with the feedback we need when we err, guidance when we need direction and the learning when we fall short of fulfilling our potential.

I am a great fan of collaboration because, without it, I would not have achieved 1 per cent of the success I have enjoyed across my business and personal life without the help of the many people who have collaborated with me.

I have deliberately created this chapter to reflect on what I describe as an inverted pyramid of collaboration.

Within the broadest section and broadest sense, we have networking, in the middle section, we have group-working and, in the smallest area, we have long-term relationships.

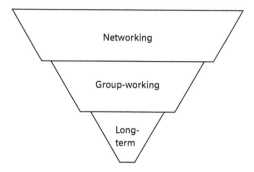

The reason for defining collaboration in this way is that, while our *network* may be significant, the people who we collaborate with daily as part of *group-working* will be fewer, and those we remain in contact with *long-term* are even less.

After a pretty turbulent 2006, I realised that I needed to rationalise my entire business, which, at the time, was a successful learning and development company called Staged Coaching.

For a variety of reasons, we decided to reduce headcount and then move our business operation from the expensive rental of a large converted barn into a smaller purpose-built facility that we owned outright.

The reduction in sales staff also meant that we had fewer people to generate potential leads and then turn those leads into new business opportunities. So, we relied on our existing network to help us instead.

We contacted all the people in our network and asked them if they could help recommend us to any potential new clients whom we could collaborate with on new projects.

Fortunately, and within just a few months, we were already meeting with potential new customers who were keen to engage us because of those recommendations!

One of these new contacts, Nick, who through doing some incremental work with us already considered us to be a part of his team, asked me to join him at an HR conference that he was hosting and suggested that it might be an excellent place for me to network.

I jumped at the chance and, without any doubt, it was one of the best career decisions I ever made for it was there that I met Tariq. Tariq worked for Visa International, within its UK HR department.

It was not too long afterwards that Tariq became a client and then a long-term friend. I worked with Tariq over several years, providing some of Visa's coaching, learning and development to managers and teams based in London and then travelling much wider afield to deliver programmes internationally.

As Tariq's career escalated, so did the opportunities to grow my business. He invited me to collaborate with him on numerous occasions, within different companies and, at the same time, was ever supportive in terms of sharing his network, his knowledge and his astute guidance.

Apart from Tariq being one of the most emotionally intelligent people I have ever met, he is also an incredible networker. He has introduced me to some fantastic and influential people over the years, some of whom have become other collaborators, clients, business contacts, and others whom I would also consider to be long-term mutual friends.

Activity

Identify a person within your current network, with whom you could collaborate on a new project, a unique business opportunity, or even just to help them out free of charge.

Think about what particular skills, knowledge or capability you might currently bring to that collaboration.

Think about what the benefits are for both you and them in developing that collaboration in the first place, and make sure that it is not just one-sided in your favour.

Now, pick up your mobile (or send an email, only if you have to) and start a conversation about how you may benefit each other. You may well be pleasantly surprised at the result.

Networking

In our online world, there has never been more opportunity for us to network with even more fellow human beings. The continuous flow of information between people from across the globe is just incredible.

Some of us will belong to various networking groups like Facebook or LinkedIn, where we comfortably share our lives, knowledge, curiosity and opinions with the rest of the world.

We are all, to a lesser or greater extent, engaging with a far broader group of people outside of our immediate *tribe* than we did several years ago.

For many, this new world is fun, exciting and rewarding and, for others, it can feel daunting and challenging. Not everyone enjoys networking. Some people prefer a few close and meaningful associates to thousands of potentially superficial ones.

Irrespective of our personal choice, we are in an age where networking is essential. It helps us to collaborate on tasks, corroborate our knowledge and find mutually beneficial relationships to better ourselves and our careers.

These benefits often outweigh the reservations any of us may have. The biggest problem, though, is knowing how and when to network, especially within an organisational context.

A strategic approach is an excellent place to start and a good fallback if we already have a network, which may not be as useful as we thought it might be and should at least help us to include the following questions:

- Why do I want to increase my network?
- What are the 'mutual' benefits of my existing or future network?
- What can I, personally, contribute to the network?
- Whom will I target and how will I prioritise this?

Once we have answered some of these questions, we then need to define our potential network in terms of access, by identifying which routes we are most comfortable using to engage with others. For example, some people may be uncomfortable networking within social gatherings, while others may feel this is the best and only approach.

There are many of these access points, and I have detailed just a few below:

- *Online social forums* – several thousand groups are online, some tailored to communities or interests, and some more general.
- *National membership* – such as institutes, federations or governing bodies; many provide memberships.
- *Conferences and business gatherings* – a great place to network in a semi-business/social environment.
- *Local Chamber of Commerce* – an excellent place to meet other like-minded business people.
- *Local business groups* – many counties in the UK have several different business groups; some purely single-sex, like working mothers and women in business, for example.
- *Local social/sports groups* – there are hundreds of thousands of these across the globe and they range from sports clubs, to litera- ture, art, science and music appreciation.

When we have taken the plunge and joined a group, it is then necessary for us to contribute in some way. That does not mean that we must start telling everyone about our life story or what is currently going on in our private lives unless the forum is expressly intended for that purpose.

What it does mean is that we must read or listen to digest what other people are saying, commenting on, sharing or expressing in terms of their views. And, only when we feel that we can add something of value to the conversation, should we make some comment or point of reference.

The online world should not be too far removed from the physical world in this regard. We have all come across those individuals who seem hell-bent on dominating a forum or conversation with their self-promoting views or opinions. Although some forums will be for this purpose, in terms of general networking, it is considered a non-conducive way of behaving.

The only thing that holds people back from contributing within a network is lack of confidence, and we should already have that sub- ject well-covered and, hopefully, ticked off on our list by now, if you have already read Chapter 3.

> # Activity
>
> Consider the size of your existing network and how you might increase this further, using the techniques we have covered so far.
>
> - What needs to change in your online or offline approach?
> - What will you commit to doing to generate more connections?
> - How will you make this happen?
> - When will you do this?

Group-working

'Being an integral part of the collaborative effort of a group of people to achieve a common goal' is an excellent place for us to start in order to discuss this topic.

Effective groupwork is about effective engagement. We need to rely on all of our emotional intelligence to help us identify the right type of engagement to help determine where people may be floundering and where they need any additional support and guidance.

We also need to know when and where we can physically ease their burden. This often requires us to be active at our task at the same time as looking out for others.

Group-work is challenging to start afresh, yet, the more that we can do it, the more that it becomes the norm for the rest of the group and, before long, our effort is reciprocated a hundred times over. That is what group-work is all about, helping each person within the team to achieve their singular and conjoined objectives.

In my business, when we work alongside our clients, we effectively become a part of their group, whether that is coaching someone on a one-to-one basis or providing an entire group of people a business consultation or full learning and development experience. It makes no difference, because the language we use, the relationships we create and the way we work is a joint '*us*'-centric methodology.

This conjoined approach encourages shared responsibility; it enables each person to go above and beyond contributing just their part of the project and, therefore, it allows the team to succeed far beyond the capabilities of any one individual.

We have all been a part of a group where people work in isolation, where 'it's not my job' is a common language and any blame for things not turning out the way expected often rests on some other poor fellow's shoulders.

Group-working is about taking responsibility for the whole group, working daily to ensure that people are part of a homogenised society. A society that relies on interdependence, as well as collective capability, will enable everyone to achieve more than they could alone.

Activity

Consider the meaning of *group-working* and how that plays out in your current world, whether that is at work or home, and then answer the following questions:

- Who is responsible for making group-work happen?
- What is stopping this from being as good as it could?
- What needs to change?
- When are you going to do this?

Long-term relationships

I remember someone once saying that, apart from our immediate family, we could count the number of very close friends that we are likely to have at any one time on the fingers of just one hand.

And, by close friends, they meant those people who, if we called them and said that we were in trouble, would immediately answer, 'I am on my way,' irrespective of wherever we, or they, happened to be at that time.

Although this might help us differentiate between a long-term relationship and a close friend, which, of course, are not necessarily mutually exclusive, it also enables us to consider what we mean by a long-term relationship.

To have known someone for an extended period is one thing, yet, to have learnt to thoroughly understand them as a unique individual is something entirely different.

We all need a few long-term relationships to live our lives to the full, not just our loved ones or those close friends with whom we have grown up.

We identify with people who are most like us and with whom we can add value to enrich, nurture and support each other.

Building long-term relationships for most of us is about having a lot in common with the other person; the same sense of humour, the same sense of purpose and, maybe, even a similar set of beliefs, values and principles.

We may find that the people we gel with most are the ones who reciprocate our help and support or those that may challenge us to become a better version of ourselves.

What we will, undoubtedly, find is that the people who are on our list of long-termers are genuine, reliable and trustworthy.

Activity

Review who might be on your long-term list of relationships, and also your close friends, and see if they are in any way different. Consider the following questions:

1 Why are they on your list, specifically?

2 How often do you communicate with them (daily, weekly, monthly, annually, every few years)? And why is this?

3 What value do you add to them as people?

4 What more could you do for them?

5 Review your list and update it, if required.

chapter 16

Innovation and creativity

What is it?

In this dimension, innovation relates to the implementation of new concepts; creativity relates to us conceiving new ideas in the first place.

The innovation and creativity dimension covers:

- Resourcefulness
- Initiative
- Spontaneity

Your dimension feedback

Use the *average* score that you recorded for this particular PEIP dimension to review the relevant feedback, as detailed by the corresponding levels of 1 to 6 below.

Level 1: Unenterprising – Negative – Contrary

You appear to be quite negative or contrary to innovation and creativity; this might be borne from not being particularly enterprising yourself or not wanting to take the initiative to come up with new or fresh ideas. It might also be due to a misguided self-belief that you are not a creative or an innovative person.

Level 2: Non-creative – Procrastinator – Doubter

You appear to be sceptical relating to any new ideas or changes, where you are more likely to doubt or find reasons why something will fail rather than work. You are most likely to procrastinate when looking to find solutions or alternatives to problems, and you will, undoubtedly, be putting off anything that may be creatively based.

Level 3: Limited – Practical – Cautious

You are pretty steady when it comes to finding new resources. However, you are cautious about unleashing any hidden creativity that you may well possess; you are inclined to find practical ways of solving problems and are genuinely supportive of others through any creative process.

Level 4: Resourceful – Assertive – Positive

You come across as being reasonably progressive in terms of taking on new initiatives and ideas, often being confident to take the lead in resourcing new concepts which you will be comfortable taking forward with an assertive and very positive approach.

Level 5: Creative – Enabling – Influencer

You are very enterprising by nature. You are often using your creative flair to influence and then enable others to develop and grow ideas for themselves. You are comfortable with a 'blank sheet of paper' thinking in addition to allowing and encouraging others to contribute to the creative process through useful brainstorming activities.

Level 6: Instigator – Inventor – Entrepreneurial

You appear to be entrepreneurial by nature; you are usually the instigator concerning developing any new creative or innovative solution to a vast number of situations or problems. You love to invent new methods, processes and even products to satisfy an identified real need that you have found.

Developing your EI in this dimension

We don't all need to have the skill sets of Leonardo da Vinci to be innovative and creative; it is already within reach of our natural capabilities. Whether or not we choose to tune in and use it efficiently will be down to individual preferences, education and the training we may have had.

The number of times I have heard delegates describe themselves as being completely uncreative and, then subsequently, go on to explain how they *imagine* that they might complete a particular task!

Imagination is that part of our mind that facilitates all the new possibilities and creative ideas that we have. As we have already discovered earlier in the book, it is most likely to be associated with the lobes found on the right-hand side of the brain, for most right-handed people.

What we do know is that imagination is initially a cognitive (conscious) process that we use as part of our everyday mental functioning. It is often associated with what is defined as psychological imagery because it involves thinking about possibilities, which, in turn, require us to recall those things that we might previously have given any space in our heads to through our sense of perception.

Imagination is not solely a cognitive mental process because, to gain any perception, we have to link our cognitive thought process with subconscious experiences in addition to a sense of time, location, objects and people.

We could, therefore, describe imagination as a form of 'whole-brain thinking', which requires us to use a different set of neurological *stimuli* from analytical reasoning and, yet, may still use the *same* neurological *pathways* to identify potential alternative solutions.

It is not what we do; it is how we do it that determines whether we are using an analytical or a creative approach to solving problems, and that is simply a matter of personal choice.

Activity

Imagine that you are on a journey to meet a friend for lunch who lives on the other side of town. An accident at the end of the one-way street you are on has brought all traffic to a standstill and is most likely not to be moving for a couple of hours.

There are several empty parking spaces along the left-hand side of the road quite near to where you are. However, the car in front of you is blocking you from manoeuvring into a suitable space.

What might you do to ensure that you still meet your friend for lunch?

The mere fact that you have even contemplated what you might do in the scenario demonstrates that you can use your imagination. If you have also found at least one solution, this will also indicate that you also use creativity and analysis to solve problems.

Resourcefulness

Resourcefulness is our ability to find different ways of overcoming a difficulty or a problem.

I often recall the 1980s US TV series *The A-Team*, which was about former members of a fictitious US army special forces unit who had escaped from a military prison where their incarceration was for 'a crime that they did not commit'.

While on the run from the military justice system, they became soldiers of fortune. They used all of their military training and resourcefulness to solve a myriad of problems for their clients.

The crazy and often humorous way they created weapons out of scrap material, adapted vehicles using odds and ends that just happened to be lying nearby, or the many other tools and equipment they made from anything else they just happened to find along the way, was a vital aspect of the storyline.

In the real world, we may not consider ourselves to have the resourcefulness or ingenuity that these fictitious TV heroes had. Although, given the right situation and then applying a certain level of creative skill or judgement, it is not something that is totally beyond our capability.

How resourceful we are in any given situation is dependent on our level of comfort; if we are comfortable with how things are, we are less likely to be innovative. Only when our comfort level is diminished, stretched, challenged or pushed, do we seek to find alternatives.

Our resourcefulness is also governed by how we think about a problem or difficulty. If we are more prone to a negative 'can't-do' and 'won't-do' perspective, there is a higher likelihood of us adopting a defeatist attitude and, thereby, not becoming resourceful.

Suppose, on the other hand, we adopt a positive 'can-do' and 'will-do' attitude. We will activate the right chemical signals and our brain will start to search for new possibilities rather than accepting the limitations within our current predicament.

Activity

Consider the following scenario:

- You are sitting alone on a fabric-covered, metal-framed chair in a sound-proofed meeting room, on the third floor of an office building.

▶

- There are three other similar styled chairs set up around the centre of the room.

- There is a window to one side, which has office-style security bars on the inside and does not open.

- There is a door in front of you, which was locked accidentally from the outside when a draft in the corridor blew it closed.

- On a small wooden table opposite the window are a pad of paper, a pen and a jug of water, with four glasses next to it.

- Your mobile phone is in another office further along the corridor.

- Apart from the standard office building electrical fixtures and the clothes you are wearing, there is nothing else in the room.

- It is a Friday evening, and the other members of staff have already left for the weekend.

Using all of your resourcefulness, now consider how you will get out.

Initiative

Taking the initiative is about using our ability to assess, initiate and do things before others do. It might also be when we encounter a situation that is stopping us from completing a task in the way we had predetermined or, through no fault of our own, when we have reached an impasse that is thwarting any real progress.

Whatever the situation, we rely on our initiative to get us through, and that often means that we need to consider all the options open to us at any particular time.

There is a widely used technique called brainstorming, which encourages teams of people to consider ideas from many different angles and perspectives. It works by concentrating on a single issue at any one time and then being open to everyone's view and opinions by removing any form of criticism of their ideas.

We can use a type of brainstorming when we are individually struggling to take the initiative.

We are likely to overcomplicate the scenario, though, introducing too many elements at any one time. So, the first job is to choose one aspect to work on at a time.

Removing any self-criticism of ideas, and by focusing on possibilities rather than issues or problems, helps us to respect our thoughts.

When we appreciate our thoughts in the same positive way that we should respect other people's, we encourage significantly healthier and much stronger neural pathways to develop in our heads, often replacing the weaker and less healthy ones.

The next internal step, then, is not to fall into any form of self-deprecation that will lead to us lacking the confidence to take the appropriate action to initiate the change we are looking to bring about.

The next step is to concentrate our initiative on what can be improved here and now. We do not have to reinvent the wheel, although I am sure that many have tried. The simple fact is that the wheel serves a current purpose and any change to its design will result in that purpose not being adequately met.

The next step is, quite simply, to focus our energy on making a positive difference to whatever situation we are contemplating.

When we use our initiative, we cannot be purely analytical or purely creative; both elements have to work in harmony. We use an analytical process to assess the situation and then the creative process to find alternative ideas or solutions.

Introducing a simple structure to support us in taking the initiative will start the analytical process. Then concentrating on one element at a time to think about all manner of possibilities, without any criticism of our ideas, allows for more radical, off-the-wall, or downright crazy ideas to surface, any one of which might eventually lead to a solution.

Of course, mental practice makes perfect; the more we use our imagination to find new ways of solving problems, the more readily we have access to that part of our brain in future.

There are many techniques you can use to help bring about a better initiative. Almost all of these will use a similar analytical/creative combined approach and, if you are struggling, it might be worth going online and searching for creative or innovative tools from sites such as Mind Tools or YouTube.

Activity

Consider using a brainstorming approach to initiate a particular change in your life:

1 What needs to change? Choose one element only and then make it a question (i.e., 'How can we improve X?').

2 Brainstorm this question.

3 Identify as many ideas as possible in, say, five minutes.

4 Do not criticise any ideas you may have had, no matter how crazy they initially appear, just write them down.

5 Focus on each idea and brainstorm how a new concept around this idea could, potentially, work.

6 Move on to the next idea, and then repeat no. 5.

7 Only move back to no. 1 when you have taken every idea through the brainstorming process and incorporated your answers.

Spontaneity

I am pretty sure that we have all met those wonderfully spontaneous individuals who appear just to eat life. They get an idea and off they go, following a new path on impulse rather than adhering to any predefined routes or rules.

We might recall those hilarious improvisation game shows on TV where the audience suggests a variety of topics. The celebrity contestants have to react by spontaneously creating a character, a story, a song or enacting a scene from the improbable, completely disconnected theme, often turning something quite familiar into something highly amusing and quite ridiculous.

We all will certainly have heard about those entrepreneurs who seem to embark on different business ventures by spontaneously following unique ideas to solve everyday problems.

For many of us, this impulsive, even devil-may-care attitude might sound a little too reckless and far too scary for us to contemplate. Although, secretly, we might dream of the possibilities of allowing ourselves to become more spontaneous, mentally free and impulsive, we always rein ourselves back to the realities of process and procedure.

So, what is most likely to be going on, and how can we become more spontaneous?

The answer is *acceptance*. We *accept* the here and now and do not challenge it because we believe that we are comfortable with our level of *acceptance*.

We *accept* that it will be someone else who takes the lead to find new ways of doing things, and we *accept* that we are not likely to change anything dramatically ourselves.

We *accept* the current rules, processes and procedures and are prepared to follow these without questioning their current validity.

Interestingly, *acceptance* is also the tool that we can use to bring about change in any situation. Take the contestants on the improvisation TV shows, for example. Before they can adapt the theme from the audience, they have to accept it, and that requires a positive mental framework.

Improvisation is all about *acceptance*. Mentally allowing ourselves to have a 'Yes, and' approach enables our creative mental juices (neurotransmitters) to flow in the direction of finding possible solutions. Denying it through having a 'No, but' or 'Yes, but' approach restricts the neurological process to just cognitive reasoning alone and, thereby, will not enable the brain to go on a search for creative alternative methods.

One of the first things that most stage and screen performers are taught is acceptance and, thereby, to expect the unexpected. This thinking enables the performers to respond more efficiently to any unplanned events that may happen in the show and then help weave that event elegantly into their performance.

This technique eludes some performers, though, as many TV bloopers-type programmes will prove. Although, when we have witnessed improvisation working well live on stage, it is almost impossible to spot the mistake or unexpected event, as it appears to be a deliberate part of the performance and then only adds to our enjoyment.

Activity

Identify a situation where you might like to become more spontaneous:

1 Adopt 'acceptance' of the situation by having a 'Yes, and' internal dialogue.

2 Pay attention to your gut feelings and react to them accordingly.

3 Identify only the positive, possibilities and potential.

4 Be kind to yourself and allow mistakes to happen without self-criticism.

5 Get on with it and have some fun!

part 3

Back to 'who' we are

chapter 17

Looking forward

We have now come full circle back to where we started, and that means taking another look at 'who' we are as individuals. Because, to ensure that we have the right preferences in place for the future, we have to be clear about who we are today, and that is all about our identity.

Our identity is the central component of our brand and vice versa. We need to remember that it represents *who* we are and not *what* we are.

It is during those impactful times when we know that our brand is fully aligned with our core values and beliefs because it becomes a true reflection of our identity.

Sure enough, we need our emotional intelligence to guide us and let us know when we are behaving in support of our beliefs and, when we are not; it should also help us to govern our behaviours based on our core values.

Our identity has to be something far deeper and more meaningful to us and to others if it is going to stand the test of time.

To nail this down, we need to consider the influence we have on other people first. We can then relate this to our beliefs and values and then back to determine how these shape our behaviours and the interactions we have.

A simple way to get started with this is to think about the various people who we engage with currently and how they regard us.

1 Yourself.

2 Family and very close friends who know us exceptionally well.

3 Good friends and work colleagues who know us pretty well.

4 Acquaintances and colleagues who do not know us very well.

5 People who do not know us at all.

Activity

What words might each of the people in these five groups use to describe us?

Find a large sheet of paper, the bigger the better, and draw five interconnecting circles in the form of a large Venn diagram and enter the positive words that each group of people from numbers 1 to 5 in the above list would use to describe you.

It is OK to enter words more than once, as there will be some cross-over between each group.

Keep it simple and try to use single words where possible and then use the model to help find the few words which will sit in the centre (at the very core) of who you are.

These are the words that define you currently; if these are genuine, they will be an accurate representation of your identity, your beliefs, and your values.

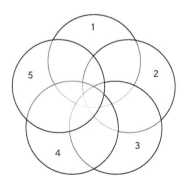

chapter 18

———

In conclusion

Improving our EI cannot be just a single, one-time investment; it requires effort, repeated practice and regular follow-up, measuring the improvements as well as developing weaker elements.

The PEIP will enable you to do this. I highly recommend that you regularly review your scores, retake the assessment to see how far you have progressed and then focus your learning on those particular elements that might still be holding you back.

I sincerely hope that the journey through discovering your emotional intelligence has inspired you to shape an improved relationship with yourself and, possibly, then lead you to have a far more rewarding relationship with every one of the people in your life.

I recall, when I was younger, that when people used to ask me what I wanted to be when I grew up, I very often just replied, 'Old!' Although, I never intended to provoke a response that some might think as just a smart-arse answer!

I just wanted to find a way of letting people know that I was always going to be a 'work in progress' and, probably also, never really wanted to identify with a final grown-up version of myself.

I still don't, many decades later. The thought of me becoming a boring old man terrifies me. I like having a childlike curiosity about the world, and I will always seek to find new ways to improve how I can interact and engage with it.

Sometimes, I fail dismally; I am just a human being, after all. Other times, I manage to transcend my mediocre credentials to achieve something impactful and inspiring and where I can genuinely make a difference.

The most significant gift that someone can bring to the world is their consciousness. I hope that I have awoken yours to the point that you will inspire yourself and others to achieve important things.

If you have found this book useful, I would love to hear from you. Feel free to drop me a line and let me know how *Discovering Your Emotional Intelligence* has helped you.

Phil
phil@philipholder.co.uk

Index